L'AMERICA

JOSEPH M. ORAZI

authorHOUSE®

AuthorHouse™
1663 Liberty Drive
Bloomington, IN 47403
www.authorhouse.com
Phone: 1 (800) 839-8640

Published by AuthorHouse 09/05/2018

ISBN: 978-1-5462-3642-9 (sc)
ISBN: 978-1-5462-3641-2 (hc)
ISBN: 978-1-5462-3640-5 (e)

Library of Congress Control Number: 2018903641

Print information available on the last page.

*This book is dedicated to my ancestors,
the Fuscas, the Fusias, LaChimias, Funaros and Orazis, whose
quiet, yet extraordinary sacrifices, have allowed me to pursue my
dreams in L'America. I thank God for His many gifts. I am also
inexpressibly grateful to my wife, Kathy, whose lifelong
support and love is as much a part of this work as I.*

BOOK ONE

Adagio con Fear

PROLOGUE

October 1915

The man squinted as the openings in the hatch delivered the thin sheets of sunlight that would certainly bring the stewards. The light was warm and piercing. At his side stood his thirteen-year-old son. He had the boy by the collar of his dirty sweater, gripping it as though his son had done something terribly wrong.

"Papa, *che cosa ho fatto*? What have I done? I'm sorry. What is it?"

But the man would not speak. And though his eyes were tearing and burning, he would not take them from that slit of light.

Finally, he heard the sound of boots. Then silence. Then the squeal of metal. Below him, the hundreds swelled toward the narrow stairs. The hatch flung open, and the man sprung to the deck, pulling his son along. They made the twenty-yard sprint to the steam pipe, the ship's gray blankets flapping behind them. He had been planning the course for hours, and this effort now paid off. In seconds, he and his son were squatting at the base of the warm metal. Here the life that was being snuffed out of Giuseppe Mosca and his son, Franco, would begin to return.

In the belly of the beast called SS *Santa Ana*, hundreds of unfortunates were huddled together. Last week they had been strangers. Today, less than a week into their thirteen-day struggle across the Atlantic, they were odd compatriots. The torrential rain and winds had made topside too dangerous. There was a rumor that one young man from Campobasso, crazed with cabin fever after two and a half days in the darkness and stench, had made his way to the deck and paid for it with his life.

Most of the travelers came from towns with no existence on the world's maps—bent women in somber garb, men in worn dark suits, children with ruddy complexions that contradicted their years, all with the same startled look. There was something different about the men, though. They were responsible; their decisions were what had led to abandoned homes and untilled fields and half-finished garments. These were the souls who had bundled up their families with determination and hope—hope now at conflict with the fear that gripped their hearts, now that they were passengers in this dung heap called steerage.

Aldo Grimaldi was not thinking of steam pipes. With his ten-year-old son in tow, he swept the deck, now covered with hollow-faced men, screaming children, and comatose women. He was searching for some sign or word of Anna. A few days into their voyage, his pregnant wife had been removed from steerage. Without explanation, stewards had placed her on a stretcher and carried her to God knows where. Aldo and Salvatore were desperate to find her.

As a steamer, the *Santa Ana* was neither better nor worse than others. She was built for oceanic crossings, of course. And she bore the scars of many voyages, her white hull now colored by the battering of whitecaps and sprays. The constant belching of the single stack had left its mark upon the once proud and shiny column. The life rafts, though never deployed, were faded and weather-beaten. Suspended end to end, ten on a side, their elliptical forms looked very much like a huge rusty chain, stretched from stateroom to stateroom along the upper decks of the more affluent passengers. These could be seen by the pitiable brood below only when the sun shone and the hatches were thrown open to allow the group above deck.

Sixteen-year-old Paolo LaChimia, a stowaway from Palermo, was making the most of this adventure. After stealing a drunken young man's uniform in Palermo, he had made his way on board, impersonating the steward. His ingenuity and cunning had paid off, allowing him to hustle his way into second class. There he had befriended Luisa Morosco, a curious teenager with a penchant for challenging her parents' authority.

Above the masses on the sun-drenched deck, the cabin passengers looked down, some with curiosity and others with pity, as they threw sweetmeats and pennies down to them. They meant well, and the treats and coins were certainly attacked by the sorry bunch, but this fostered resentment and furthered humiliation. Twenty dollars, a pittance to some, but a year's wages to most travelling below deck, was what separated second class from steerage. Twenty dollars made the difference between meals served on tables with freshly starched linens and china and slop dealt out of huge kettles and into dinner pails issued by the liner. And here the strong prevailed—the more muscle, the more slop. Above, they enjoyed the smell of perfumed ladies and musky cigars. Below, with the hatches down, breathing clean air was impossible. The stench of last week's food rotting between the floorboards and of bodily fluids lived incessantly in the nostrils of each and every tenant. Not a small number of them wondered, *Is this an introduction to life in L'America? Where the privileged live above?*

From their respective vantage points, Giuseppe, Aldo, and Paolo silently recounted the events that had led them to the *Santa Ana.*

CHAPTER 1

E migliu nu pezze e pane cu cipuli a casa tua ca storzi a la casa e l'attri.
Better bread and onion in your own home than
great feasts in the homes of others.
—Calabrese proverb

August 1915

Giuseppe Mosca, guiding an unsteady wooden cart, struggled up the winding dirt road as he did at dusk every day. And though today's cargo was even lighter than usual, he fought the rocks and crevices that peppered the two-hundred-meter rise from the plateau to his hut on the ridge. His cargo consisted of a few prickly pears, a basket of olives, some chestnuts, and one Diamante citron—one. Only a few years earlier,

Giuseppe had been shipping hundreds and hundreds of kilos of them to Livorno to be candied by the large factories there. Not so today, with the foreign markets for grapes and citrus having all but dried up.

None of that mattered tonight because tucked into the inside pocket of his jacket was pure gold. His cousin Giorgio worked as a sharecropper farther down in the valley, and the owner had had to slaughter one of the work animals that had gone lame. Giorgio had managed to talk the owner out of a piece of meat the size of his hand, and he had given half to Giuseppe. Giuseppe couldn't wait to see the look on Marianna's face. He smiled as he journeyed up the last turn and settled the cart against the wall of the hut.

Giuseppe had met Marianna Funaro at a *festa* in her hometown of Pizzoni. They had married in 1899 and settled in Serra San Bruno. Giuseppe was ruggedly handsome with a dark mustache that gave him the appearance of a man much older than his thirty-six years. His clothes were worn and dirty these days, but their fit was perfect. He cared for his appearance even under the worst of circumstances. He would never leave the hut without a jacket, no matter what the weather.

Marianna was long and elegant. Taller than Giuseppe, she would often slouch for his benefit. She had beautiful, clear skin and high cheekbones. Those who knew her had learned never to underestimate her. If a potato was needed, she dug her slender hands into the dirt to harvest it. When they were out of water, she walked the three kilometers down the hill and then back up with one full jug on her head and one on her hip. Marianna was a strong, compassionate wife and mother.

They loved their mountain village in the Calabrian province of Vibo Valentia. They especially loved to take long walks along the twisting roads where the forest was so thick that the trees formed a tunnel over the road, darkening their path. Here, Giuseppe would always steal a kiss. Marianna would wait for it, and he never disappointed. But she would feign surprise every time. He would then bend over and snatch a wildflower growing along the path and present it to her with a flourish. For a moment, they would stand and look down the road as it fell away to the coastal plain.

Then they would turn toward home again. It had always been the same. And it had always been magic. But those moments seemed so long ago.

Stefano had been born a year after their wedding, almost to the day. Franco had come two years later. Adelina had followed last. Marianna had spent much of the little girl's eight years nursing her illnesses. She was born prematurely and was so frail. Giuseppe called her his baby angel. Despite the diaspora—the scattering of their countrymen, particularly among those in Mezzogiorno, the area south of Rome—Giuseppe was certain things would improve. Even after their plot of land had gotten smaller and smaller, because of redistribution and inefficient land-management policies perpetuated rather than repaired by unification, he had supplemented the harvests with his tailoring skills. Most of Serra San Bruno knew his work. He had been the town's most notable fabric artist, which was certainly saying something, given that much of Calabria regarded tailoring as second only to agriculture among honorable livelihoods.

In time, the stitching had turned to piecework, then mending, then nothing. After all, the hunger that was rampant in Giuseppe's village—and well beyond—now defined the population. And though the residents were stubborn in their dress, they were obliged to wear threadbare vests, pants, and skirts. Occasionally, he lengthened a pair of pants or mended a lapel for a handful of *cipolli rossi*; Marianna had a way of blending the red onion with potatoes and zucchini that made the meal taste like so much more than the sum of its meager parts. But not tonight!

He bounded into their two-room hut and twirled Marianna away from the pot she had been stirring.

"Babo, you're crazy," she said. "You'll spill the water, Babo."

"I have something for you, *il mio amore*. Come see."

"Where? I see nothing."

"Reach your hand into my pocket, the one against my heart. Here." He drew her hand to his inside pocket.

She tentatively felt her way. Her fingers touched paper and then string and a bit of coolness.

"Take it out, Marianna. Take it out."

She tugged on the knotted string and retrieved the small package. She looked puzzled.

"Oh, for heaven's sake. Open it. Don't be so slow."

"All right, all right. Why such mystery? What is it?" She pulled back the string and unfolded the paper. Her eyes widened as she spied the contents. "Meat? This is meat! Where did you get this, Babo? Where?" She held it to her nose, ecstatic to find it fresh. "But this is meat!"

"So stop looking at it and cook it," he said, laughing.

She gently placed it on the table by the stove, admiring its veins and color. It was only a few ounces, but to her, it looked like a side of beef. No meat had touched her stove for more than seven weeks. "Oh, Babo!"

"Giorgio's man had to kill the brown one. It was lame. And you know Giorgio—he can talk a man out of his pants in the middle of the street on Sunday." Giuseppe looked around briefly. "Where are the children?"

"Stefano had to deliver some potatoes to Rosa and Pascale. I let Franco and Adelina go along."

Giuseppe frowned.

"Oh, be still, Babo. She'll be fine. They will be home soon. *Ha trovato piu le patate?*"

"No, no more potatoes. Prickly pears, chestnuts, some olives, and a citron."

"So we make do. We always make do."

It never ceased to amaze Giuseppe how content his wife always seemed to be—when their stomachs were full *and* when they were empty. It was always the same. She trusted God and the church. When he came home empty-handed, he would feel ashamed, frustrated, angry, and frightened, and she would touch his sunburned face with her cool and reassuring hand. "We will make do, Babo," she always cooed. "We will make do. *Il Signore e buono*. The Lord is good."

An hour later, the rest of the family sat in silence as Giuseppe prayed over the meal. "*Signore*, you have truly blessed us today. And I thank you for Stefano, Franco, my baby angel, and my beautiful bride. For the abundance of this table and the sweet smell of meat that has been gone for so long, we are thankful. Amen."

"You thank the Lord for abundance? This is abundance? And it's a good thing the meat smells because I can't see it," Stefano complained.

"Stefano!" Marianna cried. "How can you speak about the Lord that way? It is sacrilege."

"No, Marianna, not sacrilege. The boy has become an ingrate," Giuseppe said. He looked at his son. "Do you know what it takes to put this table together? No, you don't. Because you are off reading your books and dreaming and questioning your sacred heritage. I am tired of this, Marianna. I am so tired." Giuseppe moved away from the table.

"Babo, don't do this. We have meat."

"You eat it. And give the rest to Franco and Adelina. The older brother gets nothing!"

"Giuseppe!" she pleaded.

"Nothing!" Giuseppe stormed out into the night.

Adelina and Marianna were left in tears. Franco helped himself to the food. Stefano stared at his empty plate, feeling his outburst might not have been worth the sacrifice. But he knew the rules. And Marianna would never challenge her husband. So tonight Stefano would feel even greater pangs of hunger than usual. And Marianna, in deference to him, would forgo the food as well.

———————◆———————

Hours later, Giuseppe crawled into bed and pressed against Marianna. She pretended to be asleep.

"Are you awake?" he whispered.

"It depends," she finally answered blankly.

"No ... I just ... no."

Marianna turned and sat up to confront him. "This isn't working. We aren't working. None of us. And it's not your fault. I know that. But we're dying here—physically, emotionally, spiritually. We can't make it, Babo. You need to decide. Now."

"I don't know how to do this. I feel like I'm paralyzed. I'm not good with change—you know that. And this ... this is not change. It's ... Do you remember the last time our land was reduced? I stood by the new plot for days and days. I couldn't decide how to replant the rows—what to plant, when to plant. *Dio* ... I missed part of the season because I was unable—unable. How do you expect me to do this? It's too big. I'm too small for this ... for you, perhaps, *il mio amore*."

"I will not hear of it, Babo! No! Whether you stay or you go, you are not too small! Not too small!" She was having none of it.

"But how can we?" he implored. "I ... how?"

"Make a decision, Babo. The Lord will provide."

CHAPTER 2

The city of Naples was like this: wonderful from a distance, but
when seen close up, it was fragmentary, indefinable, and coarse ...
—Franco Di Mare, *The Paradise of the Devils*

N aples in the early twentieth century was a study in lamentable
contradiction. The overcrowding and disease of the mid- to late
1800s had motivated the politicos to the rallying call of *risanamento*:
making healthy again. No one argued the intent. After all, Naples was
festering. Surely a massive program of tearing down the old, rebuilding,
and relocating would stem the tide of infection and rejuvenate the city. But
some old-timers said it was doomed from the start. They blamed Prime
Minister Agostino Depretis for his bull-in-the-china-shop refrain: *"Bisgona*

sventrare Napoli! Naples must be gutted!" And the very thing designed to stem the tide of emigration actually spurred it on.

Aldo and Anna Grimaldi felt immune to the fallout, at least for a while. He was an educated man, but he had learned his trade among the dust and the stone, not in the classroom. He parted his hair in the middle and smoked hand-rolled cigars, and the shape of his mouth gave everyone who did not know him the impression that he was constantly sneering. The scars on his arms were his trophies. He often showed them to complaining laborers. He made sure they knew he was no stranger to a chisel and pickax.

Anna was the product of well-heeled Napolitani. Her parents, Carlo and Rosella Giamatti, were known to most in society. Her father had been reluctant to allow the romance between Aldo and Anna at first, but he had a keen eye for potential. And Aldo had shown potential. Anna spent a great deal of time on her appearance. It was important to her. Her blonde hair gave her a striking look of nobility. She was not a particularly pretty woman, but she knew how to carry herself, and that more than made up for what otherwise might have been regarded as ordinary features.

Not long after they married in 1903, Aldo's construction company began to take off. He was being awarded contract after contract. This *risanamento* was a good thing. After the birth of their son, Salvatore, they were even able to move closer to the bay, to Via Lavinaio just south of Corso Umberto, the embodiment of the rebirth. Corso Umberto was a wide and magnificent street, separating the port and old marketplace from the rest of the city. Here Aldo's business could be close to the action, and his stately residence offered views of the bay of Naples. Life was good.

Almost imperceptibly, soon after the move, things began to change. More and more ancient structures were being cleared away. Monuments were torn down. As each fell, Anna would question the destruction. At first, Aldo was defensive. "These things are necessary, *cara*," he would condescend. "The city will be better for it. You will see." And he would say, "Where do you think your silks and pastries and upholsteries come from? This is our business, Anna." But even he eventually began to sour.

Construction delays were on the rise, in direct proportion to the increase in brazen corruption. The phrase of the day was "*La fabbrica di San Pietro,*" referring to the thirty years it had taken to build St. Peter's Basilica in the fourth century. The saying was often repeated in piazzas and newspapers alike. Aldo was finding it more and more difficult to obtain the materials and men necessary to continue projects. His reputation began to tarnish. Contracts were pulled. Work slowed. Some of his competitors were still thriving, and that left him angry and confused. He began to doubt his competence, until he saw the pattern.

It became abundantly clear to him that a stench of favoritism permeated his industry. But the more he tried to determine the source, the more elusive it became—that is, until he ran into an old friend, Amando Batista. Aldo was a creature of habit. Each evening, on his way home from work, he would order a *caffè corretto* at the bar near his office and relax for a short time before walking home. Sometimes he would chat with one of the regulars. But more often than not, he would sit quietly and think about the day. For three years he had followed this routine, and never once had he seen Amando here. In fact, Amando Batista was known to stick close to his own *quartiere*, several kilometers away.

Amando approached him. "Aldo, my friend, how have you been?" He was impeccably attired, as usual. His high starched collar pinched a perfect knot on a perfect tie, which handsomely matched his brown and jade wool vest and jacket. Even his mustache was carefully waxed in place.

"I've been better. That's for sure. What brings you to this part of the city?"

"Business is slow for you, is it not?" Amando said, ignoring Aldo's question.

"And how do you know this, Amando?"

"Aldo, I work for the Minister of Finance."

"But—"

"No, let me be of help to you, my friend," Amando said, cutting him off. "Do you know Ferdinando Birago?"

"No … no, I do not."

"Well, you should. Here is how you can reach him."

Aldo found it curious that his friend would have the man's card so readily available. "I don't understand," he said.

"You will. Go see him. Trust me on this, my old friend. Ferdinando is a facilitator."

"A what?"

"Go see him." This time it seemed like more of an order than an offer. And then Amando was gone.

Aldo quickly paid his bill and left the bar, his head spinning with hypotheses. This was no coincidence. Amando would not have found himself in a little room of a bar on Via Santi Quaranta by chance. Of that Aldo was certain. But why? And who was this Ferdinando Birago? What business could he possibly have for Aldo? And how? None of it made sense. Dare he be optimistic about a meeting with some stranger? His curiosity was now at war with his fear.

Aldo opened the door to his apartment to find his son, Salvatore, playing on the floor with Tinker Toys.

"Look, Papa. I'm making a building like you," Salvatore exclaimed.

"Yes, I see that." Unfortunately, Aldo could not muster much enthusiasm at the moment.

"Look how big it's getting! When I finish, can we put a Grimaldi sign on the front? Just like you?"

"Show me when you're done, Salvatore. Where is Mama?"

"I'm in the kitchen, Aldo," Anna called out. "Come in here. I can't leave the stove just yet."

He found her stirring a pot. Her apron hung loosely about her, but beneath it, she appeared a bit overdressed for the kitchen. Her skirt and blouse were the kind she usually wore if they were dining out. And her hair was not pulled away from her face.

"Did I miss something?" he questioned. "Please tell me we are not going out tonight. I'm exhausted."

"No, of course not. We're staying in tonight. And I'm making your favorite—*polpi alla Luciana*," she proudly announced.

"Octopus? But Anna, it's too much. I thought we agreed—simpler dishes, not so much."

"One does not celebrate with linguine and ragu," she lectured. Then she waited for his question.

"Celebrate? Celebrate what? What have I forgotten?"

"You cannot forget what you didn't know, *il mio amore*," she teased.

But he was not playing. "Anna, what are you talking about? I'm tired. I'm not in the mood for riddles."

"You remember my aunt? Zia Concetta?"

"Of course."

"She insisted that each food had its purpose, that God gave us these for specific benefits."

"And your point is?"

"In my family, we were taught that calamari were for energy, that alici could soothe a sore throat, and that octopus was essential for a healthy first trimester."

11

It took him a moment, but finally he understood. "*Incinta*? You're pregnant? Anna! How?" He grabbed her.

"Oh, I think you know, Papa."

"No, I mean the doctor said it was unlikely. I had given up. *Incinta*?"

"There is no doubt. I waited till I knew for sure. Today it was confirmed. Salvatore is to have a brother or sister. And we are all going to have *polpi alla Luciana*."

An hour or so later, they were devouring the delicacy. There was so much laughter and conversation that it seemed there had to be more than just the three of them at that table. Aldo took this as a sign. Things were going to turn. Maybe he was making more of Amando Batista's appearance than was necessary. In fact, the encounter might not have been either chance or the manipulation of some bureaucrat with sinister motives; perhaps it was providential. At that moment, as he delighted in the spirited mood that for so long had been conspicuously absent, he made the decision. He would see what this Ferdinando Birago had to say. Maybe *risanamento* was finally returning to Grimaldi.

CHAPTER 3

Public opinion in Italy was resigned and skeptical; people greeted
news of organized crime in Sicily with apathy and distaste.
—John Dickie, *Cosa Nostra: A History of the Sicilian Mafia*

By 1915, the Sicilian economy still had not adapted well to unification.
Inequitable taxation, military conscription, and widespread
criminality threatened this tinderbox of an island. Largely as a result
of Sicily's geographic and sociologic isolation, the Italian state found it
nearly impossible to impose its laws remotely. This was problematic for
a people already ravaged by poverty. Banditry was taken up by even the
most unlikely folks. And Cosa Nostra imposed its brand of racketeering
protection almost at will. What's more, the organization was ascribed a

modest amount of credibility, with this "bourgeois Mafiosi" often acting as a mediator between society and the state.

Sicily boasted some of the prettiest foothills in the world. As a picture, Palermo was breathtaking. But its palm tree gardens, gorgeous cape, and glimmering waters stood in sharp contrast to the grime and filth of its underbelly. Here was where Paolo LaChimia had been independently plying his trade since dropping out of school. With his long hair, classically handsome face, and strong shoulders, he often turned heads, even those from superior classes. His father, a proud fisherman, had hoped Paolo would take to the family business. Every evening after class and on most Saturdays and Sundays, against the precocious boy's wishes, Paolo's father had dragged him to the docks, where he taught him about the boats and the fish and every confounded net known to man. Though Paolo was a disinterested student, he seemed to have a gift for the work. The two were known for their incessant bickering well into the night.

But his father had then succumbed to cholera just before Paolo's twelfth birthday. There were no other family members, for most had either left for L'America or disappeared into the mountains. So Paolo had taken to the streets. It wasn't long before he learned how to survive in the alleys and passageways. He found that the same dexterity his hands possessed in mending nets could be very useful in parting an unsuspecting soul from the contents of his or her pockets. He also discovered that his boyish good looks and eyes that watered on command could earn him a bed for the night in the homes of those who took pity on him. More often than not, he would be gone before dawn, his sack overflowing with their "pity."

With each passing year, Paolo's deeds grew darker and darker and his associates more and more dangerous. Though very low in the pecking order, he made his way into a Cosa Nostra *cosca*, or clan, which ran the *borgata* he called home. He gladly took whatever assignment his superior "man of honor" would throw him: picking up a package or "protecting" a shop owner or citrus grower from sabotage. The work was good. He enjoyed the intrigue. And since Sicilians were known for their unsympathetic independence, he never feared discovery. In fact, he was fond of repeating the old saying: "*Se lei la casa del vicino è sul fuoco, prende l'acqua per risparmiare la sua propria casa.* If your neighbor's house is on fire, fetch water to save your own."

This particular evening, Paolo and some friends were enjoying Toscano cigars on a curb along Via Davisi, just west of the docks. The oldest of them was Alberto, who was all of seventeen. His age and his rugged appearance gave him the distinction of being the unspoken kingpin of this little troop.

"So, Nicolo, how do you like your first smoke?" Alberto asked, chiding the youngest.

Nicolo hated the things. He felt as though someone were ripping at his throat with broken fingernails. "This is good. The life," he coughed.

"Oh yeah?" Flavio teased. "Then how come you sound like a dying Rock Partridge?"

They all laughed at the younger boy's expense.

"Alberto," Paolo interrupted, "why do you do this?"

"Do what? Smoke with babies?"

"This … all of this. You are equipped for so much more."

"Oh, listen to the big man," Alberto scoffed. "He uses words like 'equipped.' And what exactly do you do, my influential friend? Babysit cattle and lemons for Cosa Nostra? That makes you more than this? More than us?"

"No, that's not what I meant," Paolo said, backing off.

"Papa Benedict XV has been our pope only a few months now. Perhaps you can go to Rome and show him the Vatican ropes, big man." Alberto was not letting it go.

"My *cosca* is always recruiting. I'm just suggesting that your skills might be of value there," Paolo responded.

"I am satisfied with my own little *cosca*, in my *borgata* Davisi. Nicolo, Elisio, Flavio … do we not eat well?"

They nodded.

"And does the wine not happen to find its way into our bellies when we want it?"

They nodded again.

"And does the lovely Isabella not find her way to my *camera de letto all' aperto* when I am in need of her skills?"

And now they responded enthusiastically, with hoots and howls and mock punches.

"I intend to do more—much more—than what I am doing now," Paolo argued.

"Yes, well, this is a big city … and you are a very little man," Alberto spat. Without warning, he suddenly grabbed Paolo by the collar. "Don't you ever make the mistake of questioning my career path. It just might end yours. Are we clear?"

"We're clear." Paolo stood, tossed down his cigar with disdain, and walked away to a chorus of taunts.

"*Finocchio!*"

"*Faccia da culo!*"

"*Minchia!*"

Some hours later, Paolo shivered in the cold as he sat on a bulkhead and watched the lights flicker along the tiny currents of water in the port. Somehow he always found himself here. He quietly cursed his father for it. He hated anything maritime but felt comfortable only near the water. On nights when his talents were unproductive, he would find an unattended single-master, crawl under a tarp, and fall asleep to the rhythm of the bay. Why was this his music? His head told him that larger purses would eventually be his reward if he continued his internship with Cosa Nostra. But his heart found peace only along the shore.

Alberto and his crew of misfits, who fancied themselves *briganti*—there was no future there. Paolo's destiny had to be among those "men of honor" who made their living extorting the unexceptional of Palermo by day, in order to patronize the opera houses by night. Yes, this was where Paolo belonged. And he was not about to get there anytime soon, fingering the nylon and wool of trawl nets that left a lingering stench on his hands. No, his hands were meant for manicures and white gloves and the skin of beautiful, cultured women.

Tonight he would fall asleep to the sounds of swaying boats and gulls and grizzled mariners sharing grappa late into the night. The familiarity was undeniable, and after all, one more night wouldn't hurt. But tomorrow—tomorrow he would finally turn his back on this life and recommit himself to his *cosca* and the men who would prepare him for the sophisticated life of Cosa Nostra.

CHAPTER 4

Once the brooks sustained
the fields and flowers. Ginesters and little grasses
figs, loquats and pendulous grapes.
Jugs filled with pure water from the streams.

But what went wrong my children?
Why has this evil time come unto to us?
I asked the Virgin Mary
and she responded with a sullen smile.

— Dr. Tom Lucente, "Vuce e Mamma Calabria"

By the time the sun began to appear above the ridge to the east of the Mosca hut, Giuseppe was already gathering wheat and rye straw to form the bundles he needed to mend the thatch on the roof. His diligence had always paid off since the family rarely experienced leaks, and the subsequent layers now measured more than a meter in depth. There could be no doubt that his tailoring skill came in quite handy in bending, shaping, banding, and knotting the straw. When the bundles were tucked in side by side, you could not tell one from the other. The house was not much to look at, but from a vantage point on the hill that rose above the dwelling, the roof was a work of art.

Giuseppe loved this land. He loved the people. He truly felt that even in poverty Calabria offered much more than any province to the north ever could in its riches. On mornings such as these, when the sun made its way up the ridge unencumbered by clouds, he would look out over the green valley, here on the Ionian side of the Serre Calabresi range, just to catch a glimpse of the field overflowing with yellow and white wildflowers, dull green stems forcing the elegant petals toward the sun. Yes, they were *contadini*—peasants conceived by overpopulation, agricultural depression, earthquakes, and political missteps—but their poverty could never diminish the beauty of God's handiwork they were privileged to tend.

When Giuseppe finished laying the last bundle, he scaled the hill to review his handiwork. It was right. But of course, it was always right. Before heading back down, he took a moment to check out the row of poplar trees, now ten years old. He smiled. As was the custom of Calabrese fathers, he had planted the trees at the birth of Adelina, so that they could be cut down when she turned seventeen to provide a dowry. They were tall and handsome. These days he took very little satisfaction in his work, but he felt good about the trees.

Then that all-too-familiar dull ache of anxiety overcame the moment. The hut—this was all he could manage for a family that deserved so much more. The tufa foundation was brilliantly white, but it was uneven and crumbling. In their day, the limestone walls had been straight and perfect and wedged neatly into the hillside with a walkout in front that hadn't been used in some time. The livestock once had sheltered there, under the house. They were gone now—sold or eaten, at least the ones that had escaped disease. Their absence certainly made the house less offensive, but he and Marianna would trade the stench of manure for their empty bellies any day.

The living area was fashioned from irregular lengths of timber, new and old, so that the exterior was black, tan, rust, and occasionally white from the dust of the tufa. A single, small window looked out over the hill that fell from the hut to the valley below. The only door opened at the back, just above where the foundation disappeared into the elevation.

And if the exterior bore the scars of many Serre Calabresi seasons, the interior bore those of the family's wretched poverty. In the main area there was a small wooden table, a few chairs, a dry sink with a cabinet below, and a wood stove Giuseppe had been lucky enough to barter for the last of his chickens. In the center of the room was a fireplace, which offered heat in the winter and smoke in the summer to keep the mosquitoes at bay. Shelves were constructed here and there to hold anything and everything the family had. The sleeping rooms, if you could call them that, were no more than alcoves with tattered sheets that hung from the ceiling to provide some impression of privacy.

Here, Giuseppe, Marianna, Franco, Stefano, and Adelina shielded themselves from sun and rain and wind and snow, for that was all this hut was for. It was not a home. And when Marianna tried to call it that or make it that with one of those filet-lace doilies she loved to embroider, Giuseppe would fly into a rage.

"I don't want to see those in here!" he would scream.

"But Babo, they look nice," she would plead.

And then he'd repeat one of those Calabrese proverbs with which he ended all arguments, as if the quote were biblical and profound, and for which there could be no rebuttal. "*A lavare a capu e ru ciucciu, ci perdi a l'isia*! Washing the head of a donkey is a waste of soap!"

In truth, Giuseppe was a very proud man. He refused to believe that this was their destiny, that this was the life they would always live, that he was incapable of providing otherwise. "Put the lace away. You can use it in our next house. Not here, Marianna. Never here."

When Giuseppe finished his morning chores, he went back to the hut for lunch. Marianna had prepared a small plate of vegetables that she had pickled a few months ago. For all his bravado, Giuseppe appreciated his wife's sacrifices and loved her with all his heart. And no matter what the fare, he would eat it and gush over the flavor as though she had spent the day creating an exotic feast.

"Marianna, how do you do it? This eggplant is fit for a king. You should be making this in Roma. And you give it to me. How do I deserve you?"

"Oh, stop it, Babo. It's vegetables and vinegar. One of Signore Conti's cows could do the same."

"Maybe so. But still I would not sleep with the cow."

"Babo, you're terrible."

"I fixed the roof."

"And you know what, Babo? I can feel the difference already. It is very comfortable in here."

"Marianna."

"Well, it is."

Just then, they were both startled by a knock at the door—a rare event indeed.

"Giuseppe," Marianna said in fear.

"Stay here. I will see who it is," he instructed.

Getting up from the table, he moved cautiously to the door. These days, he knew to be careful. He reached for the gnarled walking stick that rested near the stove.

"Giuseppe!" Marianna exclaimed in worry.

"Stay there, I said." He approached the door, stick in hand. "Who's there?" he demanded.

"Giuseppe … it's me … Zia Annunziata," a faint voice called from the other side of the door.

"Zia!" Marianna was both delighted and relieved. "Why didn't you say so?"

"I just did," Annunziata replied as she was ushered in by Giuseppe. "You gonna hit me with that stick?"

"No, Zia … I just … No, of course not. Sit. What brings you up the mountain?"

"Zia, you want something? Some water perhaps?" Marianna asked.

"Yes, water, of course. Who told you to move all the way up here? Like a mountain goat?" Annunziata asked, panting.

"See how she starts, Marianna? Maybe you're why we moved up here, Zia." Giuseppe was only half-joking.

"So this is how you treat me when I climb up halfway to God to bring you something?"

"No, Zia. Giuseppe doesn't mean it. Tell her you don't mean it, Babo," Marianna said, attempting to make peace. "Here, Zia, have some cold water." She handed her a cup.

Annunziata was a little bit of a thing. But she packed a lot of punch, and she was respected among the Mosca clan as the matriarch. She was barely five feet tall. Since the death of her husband twelve years ago, she had worn the same long black dresses, winter and summer. They obscured her powerful legs, shaped by the hills she had climbed for most of her sixty-seven years. She was not afraid of a fight, verbal or otherwise. All of Serra San Bruno knew that confronting Annunziata Mosca generally led to defeat.

Her purse was something of a legend. It wasn't particularly large, but there was a saying around town that if you got lost in the mountains, you would do well to have Annunziata Mosca with you. The contents of her purse could feed you and shelter you for a week. From this purse, she retrieved a package about the size of a shoe, wrapped in twine. She laid it on the table.

Giuseppe reached, and Annunziata slapped his hand. "Leave it! I have something else for you right now, Giuseppe."

He drew his hand back. Marianna laughed.

"This is not a laughing matter, Marianna. You will see that in a moment," she lectured.

"I'm sorry, Zia." Marianna was now worried.

Annunziata pulled an envelope from the purse and laid it on the table beside the first package. Giuseppe only watched this time.

"Now," she said, "I have given this extraordinary thought and not a little bit of prayer. Before coming here, I went day after day to San Bruno, on my knees, to seek an answer. When it came, it was clear. There was only one answer. And it's in that envelope."

Giuseppe hesitated.

"Well, go on, open it," she said.

Giuseppe slowly reached across the table and took the envelope, holding it lightly, as though it were something fragile. He looked at Marianna and then to Annunziata for approval. She nodded.

Folding back the flap, he reached inside, frowned, and slid out a thick wad of paper lire. This was more money than he had seen in one place for quite some time. Marianna gasped. Giuseppe's hand shook.

"It comes with a condition," Annunziata cautioned.

"But …" he started to say.

"*Basta*!" she exclaimed, and he recoiled. "There is no need to count it or question me. It is a precise amount. Exactly what you will need."

"Need for what, Zia?" Marianna questioned.

"And you, Marianna, will support him in this."

"Support him in what, Zia? I am confused. What is this money? Where did it come from? What are we to do?"

"He will go. You will stay," she replied. "There is enough money there for passage for Giuseppe and one of your sons—passage from Palermo to L'America."

"No!" they both blurted.

"Stop! Both of you. You will not defy me, and you certainly will not defy San Bruno. Look at you. This is no place to raise your family. Of the Moscas left, you, Giuseppe, you are the one to carry on the name. But not here. Not in this *inferno buco*." Taking his hands, she continued, "These are not for prickly pears. I want to spit when I look at your nails, full of this mountain. You are an artist, Giuseppe, an artist. Never have I seen in my life someone who could sew like you. It is a gift, a gift from God, and you are wasting it on dirt—dirt you cannot fix. I will not put up with it anymore. You are going to L'America. You will make a way. You will send Marianna money, and she and the rest of the children will follow. And there is nothing else to say."

They sat in silence for what seemed like forever. Neither Giuseppe nor Marianna could speak. Their heads were spinning, their emotions unclear.

"It was the donkey," Annunziata finally said.

"What?" Giuseppe asked dully.

"The donkey. I sold the donkey."

"Zia, no! That was for your future," Marianna complained.

"This is my future. You are my future. The arrangements have been made. You have some time to put things in order. The *Santa Ana* leaves from Palermo in a few weeks. I like the name. It is a good sign. Ana was the Madonna's mother and the grandmother of our Lord Jesus. You can't get better than that," she boasted.

"A few weeks! Zia, no!" Giuseppe exclaimed.

"Listen to me, young man. You do not tell Zia no. You will do this for the family, for all of us. You will do this."

"But where will I go? I can't leave Marianna. Adelina is not well. Please, Zia."

"Your whole family is sick, not just the little girl. And it will be worse for you—and her—if you stay. That I can guarantee. You do this. You make a *sacrificio*. That is what a man does. Be a man, Giuseppe. Be a man."

Giuseppe hung his head. He couldn't look at his wife. He was afraid to admit his fear to Zia—if he couldn't make a stupid decision about planting vegetables, how was he going to manage this?

"I know, Giuseppe," Annunziata said. "I will take care of Marianna and the other children while you are away. That is my promise to you. And another thing—you should take Franco, not Stefano. Leave the older one with Marianna and the girl. I say this for two reasons. He's the oldest, of course. But he is very confused right now. He has one foot in childhood and the other in manhood. He is angry. That is natural at this age. But he's a thinker. And a *capu tost*. He will consider this an abandonment of the homeland. Trust me. I know this. But you must give him time."

"How will I know what to do in such a country?" Giuseppe asked.

"I said that the arrangements were made. You think I throw you to the wolves. A man, Signore Rodolfo Moretti, will meet you at the dock in New York. He is a *padrone* from Reggio. He will help you with the language, some work, and a place to stay. This is what he does. You will give him a little of what you make. You will send a little back to Marianna. You will live on the rest. In time, you will be able to send for her and the children. This is all too much right now, I know. You take some time with your wife. You hold your children. And you be at that boat, Giuseppe. You hear me?" She was insistent.

"Yes, Zia, I hear you." He was afraid to show her just how broken he was at this moment.

"The other package is biscotti. I know the children love them," Zia added.

Marianna knew, of course, that there was no other way. Just the other day, she herself had implored him to make this decision. As more and more left the mountains for L'America, she had wondered when this day might come for them. But reality hurt more than speculation. And now that Zia had intervened, well, it was Marianna's job to see to it that Giuseppe was ready to go. But more than that, she was determined to show him that she was not only supportive but also completely capable of tending to things in his absence. At the moment, though, it was all she could do to keep from bursting into tears.

◆

Giuseppe made his way down the mountain and through the quiet streets of Serra San Bruno. It was midafternoon. He wanted to take this little pilgrimage when the shops were closed and most were resting in their homes. If he could get down and back before *passeggiata* at five, he wouldn't have to speak to anyone.

The Church of Santa Maria del Bosco stood tall amid the sprawling trees that lined the grounds. Except for the Certosa, it was clearly the most impressive structure for miles. Giuseppe had always marveled at the precision with which the stones had been cut so many years ago. And the rose-colored inlays and decorative cornices were unusual. He stopped and fingered the cutouts on either side of the massive wood doors, hand-carved by local artisans. But the *chiesa* was not what Giuseppe was looking for.

He turned and descended the wide tiers of grass-covered steps that sloped away from the front of the church. At the bottom, he entered the path darkened by the thick canopy of massive beech, chestnut, and white fir trees. Finally, he emerged at his destination, the Laghetto di San Bruno. The heart-shaped pond, constructed centuries earlier, was a spiritual site for passionate believers from all over. Its waters were purported to have healing qualities. But Giuseppe's need was not physical.

At one end of the pond was a grotto and a fountain that spilled water from three openings into the pond. Several meters out into the water, a narrow column rose heavenward. Close to the column was a remarkable statue of San Bruno kneeling in the water, head slightly bowed and contrite. As often was the case this time of year, someone had waded out and placed a bouquet of flowers in San Bruno's cupped hands. This was where Giuseppe sought peace for the advancing storm.

He surveyed the *laghetto* and then slowly approached the edge closest to the statue. He positioned himself so that he could see the saint's face. Kneeling at the edge of the pond, he dipped his hands into the cool water, hesitated, and then splashed his face. Over and over, he repeated the action. Each time, he murmured San Bruno's name. Tears began to flow, but they were washed each time by what Giuseppe believed were healing waters. Too proud to cry out, he wept silently, begging San Bruno to take this away—or at least to heal the pain. For fifteen years, he and Marianna had shared a bed at the end of every day. How would he manage such an undertaking without his *bella moglie*? One last splash. Nothing. But he believed in the saint. Healing would come. Perhaps not in his time, but it would come in the Lord's time. He brushed away a combination of tears and water with the arm of his suit coat. Healing would come.

CHAPTER 5

Italy in 1915 was a difficult moment in time; life under Prime
Minister Antonio Salandra was dreadful. I know from listening
to my grandma speak about Mussolini, that the Italians were
being led down a path of disaster, heartache and disparity.
—Gary Prestipino, *Once upon a Family Time*

T he gleaming black and yellow Diatto rolled up to the front of Aldo's
apartment at the precise time Amando had told him to expect it.
The driver got out and walked to the curb where Aldo was standing
and motioned him to the back. Before entering, Aldo took a brief look
around to see if any of his neighbors were watching. He had some mixed
emotions about being seen. On the one hand, it would be good publicity
for his business. On the other, he had never been comfortable with excess.

Anna—now that was a different story. He didn't have to look up to know she was standing at the window, giggling with delight. This opulence was commonplace among the Giamattis, and she was hoping this was the first of many cars that would call for them.

Once Aldo made contact, Amando had moved very quickly. He had arranged the meeting with Ferdinando Birago in a matter of hours but had told Aldo nothing more than the time the car would arrive and to be sure he had an appetite. The driver wheeled the auto around the Piazza Plebiscito and the sprawling king's palace and headed north on Via Toledo. They slowed as they encountered a large number of pedestrians along the Spanish district. Minutes later, they were passing through Piazza Dante. Aldo glanced at the stately King Victor Emmanuel Gate, where the king and Garibaldi had ceremonially entered Naples fifty-five years earlier. Soon, they were passing by the Capodimonte museum, park, and palace grounds. Aldo made a mental note. If this meeting was successful, he must ask the driver to stop on the way back so he might purchase a delicate figurine to add to Anna's collection.

Deep in thought, he didn't notice that they had stopped on Via Gaetano Manfredi, just off of Via Miano. He was startled when the driver opened the door. "Signore," the driver said, motioning to the entrance of an unremarkable restaurant.

Aldo was a bit disappointed. When he walked in, it was rather dark, and although it was the middle of *il pranzo*, no one was eating lunch here. He had thought Amando traveled in more refined circles and had expected this Ferdinando did the same.

From a booth near the back, an arm motioned to him. "Aldo, welcome." Clearly, it was Ferdinando's arm, but Aldo would have preferred seeing all of him. He cautiously made his way to the booth. Ferdinando was seated there, already digging into a rather impressive display of antipasti. He was a tall, gangly man with a heavily pockmarked face. The cut of his suit was flawless. And everything was perfectly coordinated—tie, waistcoat, even the hat by his side, which was obviously the work of a talented milliner. "Come, sit. Don't make me eat alone."

Aldo slid into the booth opposite Ferdinando, who was preparing a small plate of the delicacies for him.

"You must try the wild boar sausage," said Ferdinando.

"Thank you." Aldo was a little flustered that they were jumping right into the food, with no customary introductory conversation. But he followed orders and started cutting the meat.

"No, no," Ferdinando scolded him. "Like this." He took a length of the sausage, wrapped a piece of prosciutto around it, and stuffed it in his mouth. "You see?"

Aldo followed instructions. It was amazing. "This is very good."

"Giorgio is a genius. I took the liberty of ordering everything. Trust me. You'll thank me. He's in the kitchen working on the guinea fowl. I'll introduce him to you later. He's one of us, Aldo. You'll like him."

Aldo wondered what that meant. How could this stranger use the word "us" when he knew nothing intimate about Aldo? What could Amando possibly have told him? But this was clearly not the time for questions. Birago was all about eating, so Aldo decided to follow his lead. After all, this meeting was occurring at Amando's urging. It was probably best to let his man control the action. So Aldo dug into the bruschetta and olives and creamy mozzarella *di bufala*. Everywhere he looked, there was something new to sample. The zucchini *alla scapece* was fried to perfection, with just the right combination of vinegar and mint. The *pane cafone* was crusty and warm. And the *soppressatta* was unlike any he had ever tasted, delicate but intensely flavorful. But his favorite was the *peperoni in padella*—sliced pepper fried with black olives and capers. He went back for seconds and thirds.

"You like the *peperoni*, Aldo," Ferdinando said. "I'll tell you why." He leaned forward as though he were about to reveal some secret. "Giorgio uses only Gaeta olives. Have you ever been to Gaeta?"

"No, I haven't."

"You must go. Eighty kilometers north. There are no better olive trees in all of Campania. Giorgio uses nothing else."

"Does your driver know the way? If we run out, I might have to go there today. I can't stop eating this," Aldo exclaimed.

Ferdinando laughed. "You're a funny fellow. I like that."

Aldo looked around. Still no other customers.

"You're looking for Giorgio's other patrons. Today, they do not come here. It's just us. I find it ... much more relaxing. Don't you think? I don't like to listen to people talking and eating and belching, waiters banging their dishes. This ... this is nice."

Aldo wasn't sure what to say. "Giorgio is very accommodating to do this."

"Yes. He accommodates me. All my colleagues are accommodating. It's a beautiful thing."

The meal continued for nearly two hours. Every so often, Giorgio, a short, stout man with three days of stubble and an apron soiled with at least as many days of use, would appear from behind a noisy swinging door with a tray full of something new—*linguine con ricci di mare*, succulent sea urchins; *braciole* stuffed with raisins and pine nuts; *cacciucco*, a fish stew that, in Aldo's mind, had no equal; and the aforementioned roast guinea fowl. Occasionally, Ferdinando would ask some superficial question about Aldo's business or offer some vague one-liner about his "colleagues." But mostly, their focus was on the food. It felt to Aldo that this was some ritual, but he was eating like a king and had no intention of interrupting the flow of Giorgio's handiwork.

"Aldo, you don't like the Lacryma Christi?" Ferdinando motioned to Aldo's full wine glass.

"I usually do not drink much at lunch. I have to stay alert."

"For what, my friend?" Ferdinando questioned. "Your business is very slow. Have some wine—the tears of Christ, shed over the fall of Lucifer. There will be no fall of Grimaldi."

This sounded authoritative. Aldo sipped the wonderfully supple red wine.

"You see?" Ferdinando said. "It is a perfect exclamation point to a perfect lunch. And we must celebrate."

"Celebrate?" Aldo was unsure. "Did I miss something? I mean, the food is extraordinary and your company most interesting. And I trust Amando. I do. But I'm afraid it is time I understand why you and he have summoned me here—and what celebration you are assuming."

"You are determined and direct, Aldo. I prefer things that way. So I will be direct as well. There is no need to recount your losses and others' gains during this difficult period in Naples. You know it all too well. You live it. But this doesn't have to be so. I can help you. We can help each other. It is true, the construction business has tapered off quite a bit since the beginning of *risanamento*. You were the fat man. Now you are thin. And you wonder about the handful of competitors who have never stopped filling their bellies. Let me reassure you, Aldo, they are not more talented than you. They are simply connected. And fortunately for you, Amando has decided to draw you into the fold. You have a very good friend there. Very good."

"The fold?" Aldo was confused.

"*La famiglia,*" Ferdinando answered. And then he proceeded to speak frankly about clans and bureaucrats and politicians, even as far as the national level. Words such as "privileges" and "protection" and "intervention" were repeated liberally. Ferdinando referred to a number of Neapolitan families who were known as power brokers in circles in which Aldo certainly never traveled. Aldo was transfixed. Ferdinando was so cavalier. Aldo did not want to appear shocked, so he tried to look impassive as Ferdinando casually cited the names and places and events that were the stuff of legend these days. He was speaking of the Camorra—Naples's Cosa Nostra.

He was giving life to the rumors. All Aldo could think about were the folk tales his mother used to read him as a child—"Biancabella," "Papa Gatto," and Giambattista Basile's *La Mortella*. It was as though he were now being told that these characters were real.

"Aldo, you are a gambler?" Ferdinando asked.

"Why do you ask?"

"You make no expression. You will do very well."

"At what, Ferdinando? At what?"

"We will start very simply. How well do you know your neighbors?"

"We're pretty active in the community. Anna is the socialite. She organizes the parties. She works in the church."

"She's a Giamatti, is she not?" Ferdinando asked.

"Yes," Aldo answered hesitantly.

"Anyway, this is what we need. The numbers in your community who seem enamored with this new Italian Socialist Party are disturbing to us. You must use your influence to return them to their senses—to the conservative establishment."

"And how exactly do I do this?" Aldo questioned.

"Your friend Amando will teach you to ... to be persuasive. He has a gift. You will learn," Ferdinando insisted.

"But ..."

"Have you kept up on the news following the earthquake?" Ferdinando asked.

"Yes. Avezzano lost 90 percent of its population—thirty thousand people. It's been seven months, and my cousin and his family have not been found," Aldo lamented.

"I'm sorry for your loss," Ferdinando said, seeming genuine. "There is much to rebuild, as I'm sure you know."

"Avezzano is 150 kilometers from here," Aldo began to protest.

"Aldo, I am not asking you to relocate Grimaldi to Avezzano. We have problems here. The Serino aqueduct has been damaged from the quake. There are many kilometers in need of repair. As it so happens, the Agency for Water Resources has made me responsible for allocating contracts. You have anything against aqueducts?"

"No, not at all. I know the work."

"I know you do. I can start you right away. The bad news is you will be looking at water delivery systems for the next two years. The good news is you will be paid for four years' work."

"I don't understand," Aldo said.

"You don't have to. Just make sure your neighbors understand the importance of antisocialism," Ferdinando instructed.

Aldo hesitated. "Ferdinando …"

"Aldo, are you familiar with *fasci*?"

"Fasci d'Azione, the new party. They were the force behind us entering the war a few months ago on the side of the Triple Entente. Intervention won over neutrality. I'm not a fan," Aldo said.

"Become one," Ferdinando commanded, raising his voice for the first time. His tone caught Aldo off guard. "See the big picture—*fasci*, a bundle of rods. You are one fragile rod, but when you bind together with others, you become strong. Decide on unity, my friend. I'll ask you what our rising star, Benito Mussolini, asked us in Milano earlier this year: 'do you want to be spectators in this great drama, or do you want to be its fighters?'"

Aldo looked at him. He couldn't speak. He felt like he needed to say something, but he was suddenly inert.

Thankfully, Ferdinando broke the silence. "It is a lot to think about, Aldo. Go home. Love your wife and child. You will do what's best for them. Call me in the morning. Go."

Moments later, Aldo found himself back in the car and heading home. He couldn't remember if he had thanked his host or even said good-bye. This was not at all what he had expected.

Aldo lay awake long after Anna had fallen asleep. She had grilled him from the moment he arrived home, and he had been able to soft-pedal the day. It had just been a business meeting—nothing definitive. Maybe they would discuss some municipal contracts in the future. Basically, he had lied. Anna was the perfect partner—so supportive, his barometer. But he needed to sort this out himself. He trusted her, but he couldn't risk being influenced by the Giamatti penchant for celebrity.

As each hour passed, he struggled with what Ferdinando Birago had offered. Four years' pay for two years' work—how could he turn that down? And that was, no doubt, just the beginning. But this deal came with a price. Ultimately, his options were clear—continue with the status quo and lose the remainder of his business and their savings or agree to work with Birago and forfeit his integrity by capitulating to the Camorra. Suddenly, he remembered his uncle Roberto Micheli and his promise of three years ago.

The rising sun lit the openings of the shutters. Anna would be waking soon. The routine was always the same. She would turn, kiss him on the forehead, draw the covers over her face, and moan that morning had come too soon. But today there would be something very different—his announcement that they would be moving to L'America.

CHAPTER 6

Zicchi e dinari su' forti a scippari.
Ticks and money are difficult to pluck out.
—Sicilian proverb

"**S***veglio. Sveglio! Il piccolo vagabondo!*" A thick-fingered hand shook Paolo by the arm. Paolo shielded his eyes from the rising sun to see a beast of a man towering over him. He cowered instinctively.

"So you like the accommodations?" the man asked.

"I'm sorry. I must have fallen asleep," Paolo feebly answered.

"My boat is not a hotel for street rats," the man bellowed. "Stand up."

He yanked Paolo to his feet. "What did you do in my boat?" He looked around the area where Paolo had been sleeping.

"Nothing. I just slept. Nothing," Paolo replied.

The man stared at him. It made Paolo feel very uncomfortable, but there was no clear path by which to run away, and the man still had him by the sleeve.

"Wait a minute," the man said as he peered at Paolo. "I know you."

"You don't know me," Paolo said.

"No, I know you. You're Tomasso's boy. Tomasso LaChimia. Am I right?"

Paolo said nothing.

"Of course I'm right. So this is how you make your father proud? You become a street rat?"

"Stop calling me that," Paolo said, standing his ground.

"What are you then? What do you call yourself?"

"Paolo," he answered.

"I know your name, boy. That's not what I mean. I knew your father for many years. A good man, a good fisherman—and proud of you."

Paolo snorted.

"Don't do that!" The man was now angry. "You must honor the memory of your dead father."

"He left me nothing. What do you expect?" Paolo countered. "And what do you know about it? Do you know what it is like to go to sleep in an apartment and wake up the next morning without it? See, that's what they do when the tenant is no longer alive to pay. They put you out."

"But you have skills, boy. I know what your father taught you," the man offered.

"Oh yes, my skills. All right then. I will work for you. You can pay me to mend your trawl nets. Or I can help you catch sea bass and cuttlefish. We will make much money. And at night I will sleep in your home after a Sicilian soup of halibut, scallops, shrimp, and haddock. Okay? Let's get started."

The man was quiet.

"I thought so," Paolo spat. "To hell with my skills. And to hell with you!" Paolo jerked himself out of the man's grasp, ran down the dock, and disappeared into the morning rush.

Paolo's stomach reminded him that he hadn't eaten in quite some time, so he headed down Via Vittorio Emanuele and turned onto Via Butera. From a bench close by, he could observe his favorite *pasticceria*. A well-dressed man was sitting at one of the sidewalk tables, drinking coffee. Beside him was a wrapped package. Paolo played his guessing game. What delicacy could this be? Cannoli? No, too early. Ciarduna? Not the right-shaped package. Biscotti? Perhaps.

He knew the routine. At some point, the man would have to leave the table to pay inside. And he was too well-heeled to take the package with him. These types always picked up their packages on their way out. So he waited. His patience would pay off, he was sure. At last the gentleman sipped his last, rose, and walked back inside. The prize still lay on the table. Paolo sprung to his feet, walked briskly by the shop, and swept the package into his arm, undetected.

A couple of blocks away, on Via Scopari, Paolo stopped and opened the package. He loved these moments—finally unveiling his reward. Settling down on a curb, he carefully exposed the contents: *bruccellati*, delicate dough in the shape of a bracelet, filled with figs, dates, and nuts. These were among his favorite treats. Paolo shoveled three into his mouth. They were still warm. This morning he had hit the jackpot. This had to be a sign.

Today he would go and see Pietro, his man of honor. He would make his case for moving up the ladder to bigger jobs and better paydays. What did that pathetic old sardine-smelling codger know about skill? Paolo's street smarts were about to make him rich.

With a belly full of *bruccellati*, Paolo made a beeline for Piazza Verdi and the Teatro Massimo opera house. Although it was a bit early for Pietro, Paolo decided to camp there throughout the day to catch him as soon as he appeared. Besides, Palermo's best piazzas for prospecting were Verdi and Politeama because they were filled with people from early morning till late at night. Here you could find some of the best freelance opportunities in all of the city.

The centerpiece of Piazza Verdi was the Teatro Massimo. This massive building, with its six huge columns in front, center rotunda, and gorgeous palladium windows, led visitors to be too casual about their belongings. Piazza Verdi was surrounded by cafés, shops, and street vendors, and the frenzy of tourist activity created opportunities for Paolo. The day was rapidly growing warm. The brilliant sunshine would attract many clients. So he didn't mind the wait for his man of honor. Between *bruccellati* and the piazza's assets, Paolo would fill the time just fine.

Paolo knew all too well that patience in his business was a most valuable attribute. Many of his colleagues possessed talented fingers, the art of speech, and a trusting countenance, but only a select few owned the stamina to say with a scheme, no matter how many hours or days or weeks it took to gain the upper hand on the target. His patience had been honed over years. This morning he applied it as he watched a particular young woman ply her own trade across the piazza from where he sat. Each hour, he moved closer, observing her labor.

She was no more than twenty, but she carried herself like a sophisticated woman of influence. She was dressed to the nines, as an Englishman who had chartered his father's boat once had said when referring to a duchess he was fond of. Tall and elegant and quite fetching, she worked that quadrant of the piazza like a professional. Finally, he moved close enough to recognize her. It was Fiorellino, meaning "little flower." That was all anyone ever called her. But he had his own pet name for her: *alla lucce della falene*, the light of the moths, for her uncanny ability to attract her prey.

It was always the same. She would appear despondent, make sure some well-dressed gentleman noticed her, draw him to her table, and spin a tale of woe until he was both smitten and unsuspecting. Then she would deftly lighten him of his watch, his wallet, or something else of value. When he left, she would move her location and resume the dance with someone else. Remarkably, she was so good at establishing her persona that when the victim found something missing, he would never consider her a suspect and return to the table. Paolo found it very entertaining. Today, she had even managed to engage an older woman.

Paolo had immediately set his sights on the ultimate challenge this morning: relieving a thief of her morning's ill-gotten gain. This was going to be fun. Paolo understood that everyone had some sort of vulnerability. He watched for hers, for that repetitive action that would leave her exposed. He carefully examined her every movement through five encounters. He found it on the sixth. At some point, to seal the deal, so to speak, she would lean over, seductively raise her skirt above her ankle and rub her foot. She knew that if her man watched every movement, she had the upper hand. What Paolo knew, however, was that this was the instant when both predator and prey were distracted. Now all he needed to do was position himself close by and wait for number seven.

It didn't take long. Seven soon sat down opposite Fiorellino and began to engage her. Paolo waited for the move. It was always to the right, and her reticule—a navy silk bag with brocade and a drawstring—hung from the left side of her chair. If she remained true to form, he could expect the move about twelve to fifteen minutes into their conversation. At ten minutes he was poised. Sure enough, at the thirteenth minute, she leaned over. Paolo's maneuver was flawless. He had the purse and was deep into the crowd in front of Teatro Massimo before she even sat up. He was only disappointed that he was unable to see the look on her face when she noticed her reticule missing. Under his jacket, he emptied the contents into his pockets and dropped the purse. He would view the contents only when he found a quieter street adjacent to the piazza.

A quick walk down Via Aragona and a left turn onto Via Tunisi put Paolo in just the surroundings he needed to savor his reward. Here, no one would pay any attention to a young man reviewing the contents of his pockets. First, he extracted an antique Pietra Dura brooch, apparently from the older woman. There was a small billfold with only a few hundred lire. Paolo knew that some of these so-called gentlemen were nothing more than posers. Next was a gold pocket watch—that could fetch something. But at the bottom of the small pile was something very special: a Giovanni Panerai watch. Over time, Paolo had come to know treasures from trash. And a Panerai was a treasure—simple in design but handmade in the designer's *orologeria* in Florence. This could feed him for a month.

Paolo returned to Piazza Verdi. After all, he needed to keep his mind on the principal task—locating Pietro and securing finer labor. In time, he spied Pietro and another fellow having coffee at one of the perimeter cafés. He pulled up a chair. *The best defense is a good offense*, he thought.

"Pietro, how is your day?" Paolo asked cheerily.

"What are doing here, Paolo?" Pietro asked menacingly. "This is not where you belong."

"I came to talk," Paolo said, ignoring the attitude.

"I'm having a meeting. You must go."

"I don't believe we've met," Paolo said, stretching out his hand. "Paolo, a ... colleague of Pietro's."

The man did not return the handshake. Nor did he utter a word. Paolo awkwardly withdrew his hand.

"Perhaps you are a bit hard of hearing," Pietro said sternly. "Leave us."

"I'm ready for better work. Please. Pietro, look, I have a Panerai," Paolo said, revealing his prize.

"So you are a schoolboy from the docks who can steal. What is that to me?"

"I want to move up, Pietro," Paolo pleaded. "You must give me a chance to show you what I can do."

"Must? You use the word 'must' with me?" Pietro was now angry. "Who do you think you are, little boy? You are nothing. And you smell like fish. And no one—no one—sits at my table uninvited."

"I'm sorry, Pietro ... give me another chance," Paolo begged.

"I am done. And you are done. Pick up your toy and go back to the water, bambino. That is where you belong."

Paolo grabbed the watch and rose from his seat. He was in shock. He looked at Pietro and the other man, neither of whom raised his eyes to him. He wanted to try to make his case one more time, but he knew he would appear all the more pathetic. Spinning away, he walked slowly from the table. He dared not look back. He knew what this meant. How could his day have begun with so much promise and turned like this? He didn't understand. After all he had worked for, in an instant, Cosa Nostra had slipped through his fingers.

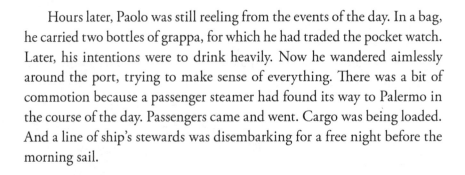

Hours later, Paolo was still reeling from the events of the day. In a bag, he carried two bottles of grappa, for which he had traded the pocket watch. Later, his intentions were to drink heavily. Now he wandered aimlessly around the port, trying to make sense of everything. There was a bit of commotion because a passenger steamer had found its way to Palermo in the course of the day. Passengers came and went. Cargo was being loaded. And a line of ship's stewards was disembarking for a free night before the morning sail.

These young men, all dressed in dark blue suits, with a single stripe down the side of the pants and flat-topped hats, were no doubt anticipating a night of revelry in the city. Paolo smiled wryly. *Another opportunity*, he thought. Most of them could not hold their liquor since they drank so infrequently. Their pockets were full of pay, and their suits made them impossible to miss. Tonight he could salve his wounds with this ship's deposits.

He watched the steady stream of them, attempting to identify his first conquest. He noticed one, about his size, who looked a little unsure of himself. The young man stopped with reddened cheeks at the bottom of the gang plank and looked about, obviously uncertain of his route. This hesitation was all Paolo needed. He approached the steward and caught him off guard by introducing himself.

"Hello, my friend. I'm Paolo, unofficial welcome party for our men in uniform." He held out his hand.

The young man hesitantly extended his hand. "Party?" he repeated, looking around.

"Just an expression. I'm here to help you find your way through our beautiful city," Paolo announced.

"And to part me from what little money I have. No, thank you." The young man began to walk away.

"Now wait a minute … what is your name?"

The steward hesitated before answering. "Biaggio."

"Biaggio—perfect. Well, listen, Biaggio, where are you from?"

"Genoa, just outside," he said.

"Makes sense," Paolo said. "I mean, the whole nautical thing. Genoa. Never been there."

"It's nice," the young man said.

"So how many times have you visited Palermo?" Paolo asked.

"This is my first time. It's actually my first voyage."

"Congratulations!" Paolo patted him on the back. "So you know nothing about our city?"

"Well, I've read some things," he offered.

"Read some things. What things?" Paolo questioned.

"About the museums, the gardens, the fountains," Biaggio said.

"Be honest with me, Biaggio … you don't care about any of that. You want to know where to eat, where to drink, and where to love." Paolo motioned with his pelvis.

"Well …" Biaggio was warming up to Paolo.

"I can show you where to get the most for your money and what places to avoid. That's important in this city. It is not all as friendly as I am. But if you have a native companion, you will be certain to enjoy your night, if you know what I mean," Paolo said with a laugh.

"What do you get out of it?" Biaggio questioned.

Paolo hesitated, in order to set the tone. Then he answered, "Someone to spend the evening with. If you must know, I'm alone. My mother died when I was very young. I lost my father to cholera but a few weeks ago. I have no brothers or sisters. And any family who has not departed for L'America lives high in the mountains. I look forward to the ships. They bring fellowship, if only for a night. And each night I spend with someone is one less opportunity for the wolves of Palermo to bite me. You do not want to wander these streets alone. All I ask is that you pay for a small meal. I haven't eaten in days."

44

"What's in the bag?" Biaggio inquired.

"Aha, my bag," Paolo chuckled. "That is my gift to you." He showed him the contents. "Two bottles of grappa. One for each. Now it is a night, eh?"

Paolo put his arm around Biaggio and began nudging him away from the dock. Maybe he didn't need Pietro after all.

Hours later, Paolo and Biaggio found themselves stretched out at the base of the Cathedral of Palermo. In a drunken stupor, Biaggio had insisted on seeing "the biggest damn church in the city." It was an impressive structure to be sure, with its arches, series of domes, huge center cupola, and tall clock tower. They had eaten well. Paolo had seen to that. And now they were well into the bottles of grappa. Paolo looked up at the clock. It was after two in the morning. The piazza was almost deserted. Biaggio was in and out of consciousness and unaware of anything.

Finally, Biaggio gave up the ghost and passed out for good. Paolo immediately began digging through his pockets. He was disappointed at the contents. He sat back and looked at the young man. He almost felt sorry for him. But he shook off this feeling as the grappa talking and resumed mining for belongings. He located Biaggio's billfold. Leafing through it, he found the ship's ID: the SS *Santa Ana*. He carefully read the documents and looked again at the young steward lying in the shadow of the cathedral. This was the sign. *Ringrazio Dio*, he thought. His hands were shaking as he removed Biaggio's pants.

CHAPTER 7

When we are children, when we are young, it is natural to love
our friends, to be generous to them, to forgive their faults. But
as we grow old and have to earn our bread, friendship does not
endure so easily. We must always be on our guard. Our elders no
longer look after us, we are no longer content with those simple
pleasures of children. Pride grows in us—we wish to become great
or powerful or rich, or simply to guard ourself against misfortune.
—Mario Puzo, *The Sicilian*

Paolo hurried along Via Emmanuele Paterno, running east along the
river. His gait was awkward because Biaggio's boots were a little
small. The uniform fit pretty well, however. And with the hat perched
on his head, he actually felt a bit regal. Soon, he arrived at the garden in

the open area between Via Giuseppe Bennici and Buonriposo. Ponte dell' Ammiraglio and its span of seven arches crossed a riverbed that had been dry for centuries. From a distance, the bridge appeared relatively intact. But Paolo knew better.

He crawled under the second arch, making his way to the center. It was very dark, but Paolo could find the spot in his sleep. He felt along the rough-hewn stones until his fingers crossed an area of broken mortar. Pulling out five stones, he revealed his store. Tucked about a meter inside was a paper valise. Paolo stretched his arm to the limit and yanked it out. Here is where he kept his belongings safe—some extra clothes, the remaining rewards of his pickpocketing, some dried beef, towels, a few tools. He emptied his pockets into the bag, closed it, and slid back out of the arch.

For a moment, he studied the ancient bridge—Admiral's Bridge, named after some old guy a long, long time ago. Paolo had no use for history. But he did believe in fate. And he felt like an officer in his new uniform. Admiral it was. After all, soon he would be walking the same floor as an admiral. Uncommon melancholy suddenly overcame him, even a trace of fear. He was leaving Palermo, Sicilia. This cruel city had brought him more trouble than a sixteen-year-old should witness. On a good day—and there weren't many of those—he filled his belly and slept warm. But the others?

No. This was right. He felt sorry for young Biaggio, lying back there in the piazza. He would awaken with a disorienting headache and sick as a dog. But it could have been worse. Paolo could have left him near naked, but he had reconsidered and replaced the uniform with his own dirty clothes. And he had left the Panerai in one of the pockets. The boy was naive but not stupid. He could pawn the watch and make his way back to Genoa. Paolo slung the valise over his shoulder and headed back to the docks.

When he arrived at the *Santa Ana*, all was still relatively quiet. He hid behind a stack of cargo, not wanting to reveal his stolen uniform just yet. There had to be a plan. He knew he couldn't just saunter up the gangplank like he belonged. Even with Biaggio's identification, there might be some suspicion. So he waited.

Soon, he heard some commotion coming from the east. He carefully peered around the stack to see a group of about ten or twelve stewards, obviously drunk, returning to the ship. They were singing and hitting each other and laughing. As they passed the cargo, Paolo jumped in behind them. The unsteady band staggered up the gangplank. At the top, they were stopped by someone in authority. Paolo couldn't see, but the man was lecturing the group and asking for their papers. They all fumbled for their billfolds. There was some pushing and shoving. Those at the front of the group—those who didn't drop their wallets—flashed their identification after some delay. Paolo was ready to turn and run when the man suddenly shook his head and waved them all aboard.

Before he knew it, Paolo was on deck, following the lead of the others. He remembered Biaggio's description of the forecastle, where all the stewards had small assigned bunks and a single chest for personal items. When they finally found their way there, Paolo hung back, watching as the sorry lot collapsed one by one into their little spaces. As the last one fell, Paolo spied an empty bed, which he assumed to be Biaggio's. He ducked into it, pulled the thin gray blanket over him, and thought about his next move.

Paolo knew from those who had traveled to L'America and back that the best place to disappear was steerage. On the way to the forecastle, he had seen a directional sign for it. He memorized the route so that he could make his way there when the opportunity arose. Once there, he could stash the uniform, change into his own clothes, and huddle with the masses for the voyage west. How difficult could this be? Surely the hard part was over.

Throughout the next couple of hours, Paolo fought the urge to sleep. He knew that if he closed his eyes, the night would get away from him. This was strange territory, so he could not let down his guard. In the morning, the steamer would depart for the three-hundred-kilometer trip to Naples. It would overnight there, take on more passengers, and then leave for the two-week voyage to L'America. He had learned all this during his hours with Biaggio, who, it seemed, did not understand the meaning of silence. At the time, it had been maddening. But the incessant chatter from the young man was now paying off.

Eventually, Paolo began to hear the sounds of sandpipers, larks, and terns. It was the hour before dawn. Many nights, after filling his sack with a compassionate woman's silver, he had lain awake in a guest room, waiting for the birds. The minutes before dawn provided the greatest chance for successful escape. And so it was here. He quietly gathered up his valise, slipped out of the cramped bed, and made his way to the deck. He was an expert at the silent walk. It didn't matter the shoe or boot; he had perfected the art of soft feet. Unnoticed, he found a hatch to steerage, opened it, and descended.

Paolo was unprepared for the smell. He lived by his senses and was very good at isolating them and using them to his advantage. But here, the odor almost incapacitated him. He needed his eyes to adjust to the darkness, his ears to identify the surroundings, and his touch to maintain his stability. And now, they were all instantly compromised by the stench.

In time, he gathered himself. He was able to see well enough to know he was alone. He had expected passengers. After all, he needed to hide among them. This was all wrong. Where could they be? Given the smell, maybe he had misread the sign and wandered into some garbage compartment. Reading was not his strong suit. Still, there were rows and rows of two-tiered tiny berths—metal frames with yellowed cotton drapes. The beds were two-thirds of a meter wide, with less than a meter of height between them. Each had a thin mattress, a blanket, and a straw-filled pillow. He noticed that only about half of them had life preservers. Suddenly, someone touched his shoulder, and he spun around defensively.

"*Calma*," a tall uniformed man cautioned him. He had stripes on his shoulder, so Paolo assumed the worst. "You look like someone who is seeing steerage for the first time. This your first sail, young man?"

"Yes … yes," Paolo stammered.

"Get used to it. This is the best it's going to smell. Wait until we're a week out. Then you will long for today," the man said with a smirk. "Well, since you are already up, you might as well rinse down the floors. Grab a bucket and start bringing seawater from the bilge. Just do the best you can. This is steerage. The occupants are nothing more than cargo with legs. You will see that soon enough when they board in a few hours. And put your valise in your berth. You can't be carrying it all over the ship with you." With that, the man turned and left.

Paolo stood for a moment, watching after the gangly officer. He allowed himself a wry smile. He hadn't expected discipline on a steamer to be so casual. Maybe he would make use of the uniform after all. He had a pretty good idea of the layout of a ship. His father hadn't tutored him only about small fishing vessels. Every time a passenger liner docked at the Port of Palermo, he would point out the parts of the ship and later test Paolo. That was his idea of fun. He had even made Paolo memorize the different liners' flags, which flew high above the deck. Paolo had noticed the *Santa Ana*'s right away: rectangular, with a blue cross, a white border, and a blue upper quarter at the hoist, with a red "I" in a white, six-pointed star—Italia Lines. Carting buckets of water would be a small price to pay for passage to *il nuovo mondo* on a steamer where the crew spoke Italian.

No one paid much attention to the young steward hauling bucket after bucket to steerage. Occasionally, he would get a nod, which he returned cheerfully. This lower deck, next to the engine room, was one huge conglomeration of bed frames with communal washrooms at either end. The smell improved with each toss of seawater. He was thankful for that. As the sun rose higher in the sky, there was more and more activity topside. Cargo was being hoisted on board, and passengers were finally making their way up the gangplank. Paolo occasionally stopped to watch the small pre-boarding areas set up on the dock where doctors examined the travelers. Occasionally, a distraught man or woman would be turned away and denied passage for one physical reason or another, and a commotion would ensue. The authorities would be called, and the screaming would-be passenger would be hauled away by angry *polizia*, who seemed, at least to Paolo, to delight in this.

All this reminded him of the stories he had heard about what the new arrivals were subjected to before and after disembarking in L'America. He definitely needed a plan for that. But he had a couple weeks to figure that out—if he made it past Naples. First things first. He needed to take advantage of the two hiding places he now possessed on the ship. One was established—Biaggio's berth in the forecastle. Now, before all the Palermo passengers boarded, it was time to stake his claim to one in steerage. He sought out a lower berth, not far from a washroom. He took a towel and shirt from his valise, draped them over the metal frame, and tucked the paper luggage under the blanket. This would do just fine.

◆

Giuseppe Mosca and his son Franco sat on their trunk in the middle of the mail boat as it neared the Port of Palermo. Mercifully, the winds and swells had died down, preserving the contents of their stomachs. An hour earlier, this was not the case. It had been all they could do to keep their last meal down. Franco's face spoke volumes, and Giuseppe could offer little consolation.

"Zia Annunziata was very good to do this. You must understand, Franco. This is best."

Franco was not convinced. "Papa, more than a day ago, we left Mama, Stefano, and Adelina on the side of a mountain. My mother and sister could not even say good-bye, their wailing was so loud. And did you see my brother? Did you see how angry he was?" Franco moaned.

"Before he was resurrected, our Lord had to suffer," Giuseppe said. "We can do this much for those we love."

"My bottom is very sore," Franco said as he squirmed. "I thought we were traveling all the way to L'America by horse cart."

"Yes," Giuseppe said, patting him on the cheek. "Me as well. But Zia made all the arrangements. And we must be thankful. I did not know that Reggio Calabria was so far from Serra—nearly eight hours. I am sore too."

In the distance, the morning mist was lifting to reveal the city of Palermo. Giuseppe had never seen so many buildings, all climbing the hills that fell to the water. There were so many boats, so many gulls. The mail carrier made a slight adjustment in its route and headed straight for the port. That's when both father and son spied her.

"Papa! Papa! Do you see?" Franco cried.

"Yes, yes, I do. That must be her," he said. He looked at the black letters and then pulled some papers from his jacket pocket. He struggled through them to find the letters. They were the same: SS *Santa Ana*.

For several minutes they stared in awe at the size of the steamer. Over the past few weeks, they had imagined the journey, of course. But no matter how grand or how fearful their dreams, neither of them had pictured such a structure.

"How many of us will be going, Papa?" Franco asked finally.

"I don't know, my son."

"Guess then," Franco said.

"All right." Giuseppe thought for a moment. "Do you remember the last time we went to the Feast of San Bruno? When we all gathered around the *laghetto* for prayers?"

"Yes, of course."

"Well, perhaps that many. Didn't you practice your mathematics that day by counting them?"

"Yes!" Franco said, suddenly remembering.

"Then you tell me how many."

"One hundred and seven," Franco announced.

"Well, one hundred and seven it is," Giuseppe declared.

"Imagine, Papa, one hundred and seven on one boat!"

Giuseppe tucked the papers away. In another pocket he sought out the only picture of Marianna he carried with him. "We must trust *il Signore, il mio amore*," he whispered to the image. "We must."

◆

Several hours later, the berths in steerage were about a third full. Nearly a hundred pathetic souls were trying to make sense of their temporary home. Most had never seen anything like this. No matter how poor they were, they had never really experienced this feeling of claustrophobia. In Mezzogiorno, the mountains and countryside could always be refuge to families who lived in overcrowded apartments and mud huts. Those with their wits about them worried about what space would remain after the ship took on more travelers in Naples.

Some took very little time to show the effects of this stress. Fights broke out between patriarchs, who attempted to protect their own. Others huddled together, exhausted and frightened. Many were afraid to leave their belongings after settling in, so they did not join the throngs on deck who wrestled for a last peek at the families they were leaving behind.

The Moscas had made their way through the examination or, as Giuseppe referred to it, the humiliation. Franco hadn't liked lifting up his shirt for the uniformed doctor. Now here they were, in the darkest recesses of the ship, sitting on their hand-carried bags and wondering how this place could exist inside such a beautiful exterior. At first, Giuseppe had thought this might be another holding area—that is, until he saw the berths and the blankets and stared into the hollow faces of his fellow passengers.

◆

A loud screech announced the initial turn of the enormous screw in the engine room. There was a collective gasp on board. The sound scared some of the children, who began to cry, along with parents and older siblings who were facing the pain of separation. Paolo, still in uniform, positioned himself against a rail on the deck and watched the growing distance between him and the dock. The ship's movement was smoother than he had expected. But then again, he had never been on a vessel larger than fifteen meters in length. Maybe he got caught up in the emotion on board. Maybe it was the wind and salt spray. But he found himself wiping away tears that were suddenly streaming down his cheeks. He quickly regained his composure. After all, crying was not becoming of a steward.

CHAPTER 8

"There is in the DNA of the Italians a bit of madness,
which in the overwhelming majority of cases is positive. It is
genius. It is talent. It's the masterpieces of art. It's the food,
fashion, everything that makes Italy great in the world."
—Matteo Renzi

T he sun broke through overnight clouds high above Mount Etna, but
the lot in steerage was unaware. There the only light was artificial, and
it was insufficient. Giuseppe Mosca turned uncomfortably in his berth.
He was not a large man, but the mattress, if you could call it that, barely
supported his small frame. To make matters worse, he had been instructed
to keep all his hand baggage off the floor. There were no hooks or shelves,
so his belongings occupied the same space that he did. Some he placed

on Franco's berth, but they also had to keep with them the two tin plates, cups, and sets of utensils that the liner had issued them for the voyage.

By the sound of increased foot traffic and cargo activity topside, Giuseppe suspected the Naples passengers would be arriving soon. He prayed that some berths would remain vacant so that they could spread out a bit once they were underway.

Franco stirred in the berth above him. "Papa, what is all that noise? Have we arrived in L'America? I want to see." He jumped down and shook Giuseppe. "Papa, get up. Let's go see L'America!"

Giuseppe sat up and put his hands on Franco's shoulders. "Franco, you must be patient. We are only in Naples. After we take on more travelers, we will be on our way. Don't you remember? I told you that the trip would take thirteen days. We left Palermo only eight hours ago."

"Then let's go see Naples," Franco pleaded.

"No, my son. Soon more passengers will take their places down here. We must protect our things. There will be plenty of time to go up on the deck. Just not today," Giuseppe softly instructed.

Franco folded his arms and turned away, pouting. "It's dark in here."

"Soon they will open the hatches for the new passengers. Then you will see the sun."

"When will we eat?" Franco asked.

"I don't know. They will tell us. Mama packed some dried biscuits in your bag. Why don't you find them?"

"I don't want biscuits."

"Suit yourself. But Franco, if you start your journey in such a state, how will you arrive? You must be a man now. Do not show the child. Remember, *cume ti vidanu te descrivanu.*"

"I know, Papa. I know. As they see you, they describe you," Franco acknowledged.

"Come. We will eat the wonderful biscuits Mama prepared for us. And we will give thanks to *il Signore* for His provisions."

Franco climbed up to sit alongside his father, pressing against him on the side of the berth. The tin plate and cup Giuseppe had stored beneath the mattress rattled under him. They laughed. Franco bounced to make the noise again. Again they laughed. Giuseppe kissed his son on the forehead and held him close. There would be plenty of time for fear. For now, biscuits and laughter were exactly what they needed.

◆

Aldo held fast to his wife and son as they slowly snaked their way through the line of passengers waiting to embark. On this gleaming morning, the Port of Naples had been transformed into a small nation. It seemed to Aldo that each passing hour brought scores more people. Everywhere he looked, huge nets were filled to overflowing with trunks and valises. A little more than an hour ago, he had abandoned his attempts to keep their own checked baggage in view. At this point, it was all he could do to manage Anna.

"That man's bag of cheese keeps brushing against my skirt. I'm going to smell like *scamorze* all the way to L'America," she complained. "Shouldn't we be in a different line?"

"What sort of line are you referring to, dear?" he asked.

Anna bristled. "A line with different people, Aldo."

"Oh, I understand. You're looking for the Giamatti line." This was not the morning to try his patience.

"I told you to call my father. He would have made arrangements," she chided.

"Your father does not support emigration. You know that. Especially when it involves his youngest daughter. I am a villain now."

"Well, what do you expect? Salvatore, stay close to me. I don't want you catching anything," she said, pulling at her son's jacket sleeve.

The three of them looked well-groomed because Anna had insisted they dress well for travel. Aldo wore a dark suit, a white starched shirt, a black tie, and a felt bowler hat. Anna had opted for a skirt layered in white and royal blue and a shawl she could pull over her head to protect her hair. She wanted to make this something special for Salvatore, so she had dressed him in mid-calf navy pants, a three-button navy jacket, high boots, and a hat with a metal band and medallion that made him appear nautical. Of course, there were multiple changes of clothes in their hand baggage.

"When we settle in our cabin, we will all need to wash our face and hands. I've heard tales about diseases, and we can't be too careful," Anna instructed.

"There is no cabin, Anna. We're traveling in steerage," Aldo said.

"What does that mean?" she questioned.

"When I saw the price difference between the cabin classes and steerage, I decided we will need the money more in L'America than we need to throw it away on luxuries here," Aldo explained.

"Are you telling me we don't have a private room?" she challenged.

"We will be fine, Anna. This is best for our future."

"Aldo, I'm pregnant. I need my privacy."

"It's thirteen days. And I'm sure you will have privacy enough. We must all sacrifice in the short term to benefit later." He was suddenly feeling defensive. What if he had made a mistake? After all, it wasn't as though they couldn't afford it. Still, the sale of their belongings in the weeks leading up to today had not brought nearly as much as he had hoped. He was afraid of the months that lay ahead. His uncle Roberto had encouraged this move, but he also had warned Aldo that the family's experience of joining him in L'America, though full of promise, would be financially challenging for them all.

After what seemed like an eternity, the three were finally making their way up the gangplank and along the deck of the SS *Santa Ana*. Some of the delay had been a direct result of Anna insisting on seeing someone in charge when she was asked to subject herself to a superficial examination.

"I don't care how superficial it will be," she had argued. "I will not have some would-be physician in a steamer uniform pawing at me. I demand to see a real doctor." After a wait of thirty minutes, a Port of Naples physician supervisor had personally attended to Anna, and the three had been cleared for travel.

Still protesting the examination and the fact that she had to carry her own hand baggage, Anna negotiated the metal stairs that disappeared into the darkness of steerage. At the bottom, they were carried along by the throng of passengers, past row after row of pathetic berths, already filled with hundreds of souls. Anna said nothing. In truth, she was unable to speak. Horror and fear had choked her to silence.

Aldo assessed the situation in short order. If they were to find appropriate space, he had to move the three quickly and decisively. On the port side, he found a row of berths with a narrow passageway running between them and a ship's wall. He pushed Salvatore onto one.

"Don't move," he said sternly.

Salvatore was confused, but he obeyed the instruction.

He then grabbed Anna's hand baggage and tossed it onto the berth above.

"Aldo, be careful with that," she protested.

He ignored her and sat on the berth immediately next to his son. In an instant, the berths around them, as far as they could see, were claimed by belligerent passengers wrestling for their own spaces. Some fought. Others wailed. Aldo held his family close until things began to settle.

"These are our beds," he said finally. "Place all of your things on the mattress. Let nothing touch the floor. Do you understand?"

Anna was frightened by his tone. He rarely spoke harshly to either of them. She worried that he knew something he wasn't telling her.

It was nearly impossible to talk above the din. But Aldo felt it was imperative to establish ground rules. And so he began to shout instructions. "Talk to no one, unless they are wearing a ship's uniform. No one. Avoid eye contact. Touch no one. Neither of you will leave your berth without me. We walk together. We sit together. We sleep together. Anna, when you need to go to the washroom, Salvatore and I will accompany you and wait outside the door until you are finished. Am I clear?"

They both nodded mechanically.

Aldo surveyed their surroundings. This was not at all what he had expected. Although most of the passengers were Italian, the strange assembly of nationalities and the drone of voices evoked a kind of Babel. There were Russian Jews, Irish farmers, Greeks, people strangely attired in kilts, Arabs in long robes, and even Cossacks with terrifying scowls and long, curved swords that hung from their belts in ornate sheathes. Thirteen days suddenly seemed like an eternity.

Paolo made his way past the army of travelers, down the stairs, and around the corner to the berth he had claimed in steerage. This was a mistake. Every meter or so, he was confronted by angry or confused passengers vying for his time and assistance. Ignoring them further enraged the already agitated bunch. And for each one he placated with an empty promise, ten more accosted him. Clearly, this would be the last time he wore the uniform in steerage.

He dug under the mattress to ensure that his valise was still safe and secure. He decided to disappear here for at least the start of the trip. So he gathered a few clothes, tucked them under his arm, and headed for a washroom. There he took advantage of the uniform one last time, cut to the front of the line, and elbowed his way into a stall. Paolo quickly changed, forced his way back out, and returned to his berth, where he stashed his steward garb. As he lay back on the mattress, he felt a now familiar shudder as the ship pulled away from the dock. Confusion and fear lodged in every corner of this dungeon. Yet he felt oddly at peace—an island of contentment in the midst of chaos.

CHAPTER 9

For many, the steerage passage across the Atlantic was remembered
as a kind of purgatory, a period of punishment imposed on them
by Providence for having abandoned their motherland.
—Jerre Mangione and Ben Morreale, *La Storia*

"**P**apa, I'm going to be sick," Franco moaned.

Giuseppe sat next to his son and tried to console him. But
in truth, he was just as nauseous himself. Not even two days into their
trip, both were suffering from seasickness. The constant rolling that was
inescapable in steerage was more than they could bear. For the last two
hours, Giuseppe had been calling out, hoping a steward would be able to
help them. But none could be found.

"Papa, please help me," Franco begged. "Where are they? Why don't they come?"

"I don't know, my son. I don't know." Giuseppe felt so helpless.

A couple of rows of berths away, arguing could be heard. Apparently, a Greek and a Russian were pulling on a ship's blanket, each claiming ownership. In their native languages, they cursed and threatened each other while members of their clans surrounded them with shouts of encouragement. As the scuffle escalated, two stewards appeared in an attempt to mediate. If not for the seriousness of the situation, the scene might have been humorous—a furious battle between a Greek and a Russian and two Italians attempting to negotiate a peace. There was a lot of passion and a lot of rhetoric and no comprehension.

The conflict was finally resolved when one of the stewards produced a second blanket. As the group dispersed, Giuseppe shouted out to the stewards.

One of them approached him. "Can I help you, sir?" he asked.

"Yes, yes, of course," Giuseppe said. "Please, my son is sick. Can you help him?"

The steward suppressed a smile. "What would you like me to do, sir?" he asked.

"There must be a doctor on board."

"Of course. And if he tended to the seasick, he would have no time for those who are truly sick," the steward explained.

"I don't understand. My son is sick," Giuseppe pleaded.

"What your son has is temporary. The only remedy is dry land. That you will have in eleven days. In the meantime, encourage your son to vomit. That should make him feel a bit better."

"But the weather …" Giuseppe said.

"Use the floor. That is what you do in steerage. Deposit it as close to the edge of your berth as possible. That way you can shovel it underneath." With that, he disappeared.

Giuseppe could not speak. He turned to comfort his son, but Franco was now bent over, heaving violently beside his berth. After several moments, Giuseppe was unable to hold his own, and he joined in his son's misery.

———————— ◆ ————————

Unbeknownst to the sufferers in steerage, the mighty ship slowly made its way through the Strait of Gibraltar, passing between Cape Marroqui to the north and Cape Malabata to the south, a width of only thirteen kilometers. Leaving Spain and Tangier behind, it steamed out into the open sea. The fortunates in first and second class pressed their faces against portholes to see the rocky coastlines. Some even clapped as the last evidence of land disappeared behind them. Though the weather was bleak, their hearts were full of anticipation.

Guido Morosco, a young attorney from Naples, sat and smoked as his wife, Antonia, and fifteen-year-old daughter, Luisa, smiled through the windows at the landscape. Guido was a short but confident man, with a thin mustache and a receding hairline that he often complained about. Antonia was beautiful and dark. Luisa had her mother's skin tone and radiance and Guido's self-assurance. From early on, the two had worried about their daughter's lack of fear and headstrong behavior. They hoped L'America would tame her.

Guido brushed away the ashes that had fallen from his cigar and smoothed the tablecloth in front of him. The dishes had been cleared. The passengers had just finished a surprisingly scrumptious dinner of haddock, risotto, and roasted peppers. His espresso had gone cold, and he looked about for a waiter to replace it. The closest one was several tables away, laughing with a foursome who happened to be taking their game of *scopa* very seriously. Cards were thrown in mock anger, and their glasses of amaretto rattled about the table.

When Antonia and Luisa returned, he motioned to them to sit. "Do you hear that?" he asked.

"What?" Antonia responded.

"The music," he said. "They have an orchestra upstairs."

"Of course they do," Antonia replied. "It's first class."

"We have nothing but the sound of old men playing cards," he complained, "and cold espresso. At these prices I should at least be able to get a refill without shouting at the top of my lungs. The man is ignoring me."

"Papa, you should have seen the rock," Luisa exclaimed.

"What rock?" he asked.

"Gibraltar—the Rock of Gibraltar. It was just like in my geography book," she said.

"So at least you look at the pictures in your textbooks," he chided.

"And now we are in the Atlantic Ocean. Water as far as you can see." Luisa was clearly ignoring the sarcasm. "When will we be able to go outside?"

"A steward told me that the weather out here is unpredictable. The rain could be with us for hours or days," Antonia lamented.

"But I want to stand on the deck. If we're on a ship, we must stand on the deck," Luisa complained.

"That is not possible right now," Guido instructed.

"But I have a coat, Papa. I've seen others."

"And they don't have the sense God gave them. You will stay inside." He was emphatic.

"Then may I have some of your grappa?" Luisa asked.

"No. You had some sips of wine at dinner. That is enough," he said.

"But Papa ..."

"No."

"Guido, what is the harm? Let her have a little."

"A sip, but that is all," he said, pointing to his daughter.

Luisa slid his glass to her, looked at the contents, and then looked at her father. The glass was nearly full. She briefly assessed the situation, raised the glass to her lips, and swallowed it all. She tried in vain to suppress a cough.

Antonia feigned anger.

Guido was clearly disgusted. "You see, Antonia? You see?"

Twenty minutes after the dinner bell sounded, Paolo was still in his berth, watching the chaos develop around him. As hungry as he was, he couldn't bring himself to eat. He had heard someone talking about the potatoes and unrecognizable meat, but the way the stewards slopped it onto the metal plates of those standing in line, it looked like gruel. His fellow countrymen picked through it, happy to have anything. Fearing the food was not kosher, the Russian Jews refused it, opting for the pickled herring, black bread, and tea they had brought with them.

The Slavs, however, ate anything and everything. But it was the way in which they ate that turned Paolo's stomach. Apparently, utensils were uncommon in the Balkan Peninsula, for it seemed that the Serbians, Albanians, and Bulgarians had no use for them. Rather, they scooped their food with their hands, pressed it deep into their mouths, and licked and sucked the remains from their fingers. Many of them fought over the bits and pieces that fell to the floor. They were loud and gruesome and disgusting.

When he couldn't take a moment more, Paolo reached under his mattress for the uniform. He'd take his chances making the switch again to be clear of these animals. It wasn't hard to change clothes. In the midst of this feeding frenzy, no one noticed the young man who turned steward. After stuffing the civilian garb under the mattress, he hurried up the stairs, dodged the wind and rain, and found second class. He made his way to the dining room and was disappointed to see the tables cleared. Undeterred, Paolo pushed through the swinging doors that led to the kitchen.

"You're late if you're looking for food," one of the cooks said.

"I got very busy. There must be something," Paolo answered.

The cook opened a door to one of the coolers and pulled out several plates. He set them down on a large cutting board. "Here, but don't expect me to serve you."

Paolo unwrapped the gifts—haddock, risotto, potatoes. He found a fork and quickly began downing the delicacies. Then he remembered the Slavs and slowed down. The fish was tender and the risotto buttery. The potatoes, though cold, were still crisp. His fear of detection was quickly dissipating. Clearly, he needed to spend more time in uniform. The benefits far outweighed the risks. He had always been resourceful. He trusted his instincts, though now they were a bit compromised by the food.

After filling his belly, he returned what remained to the cooler. He looked out the round windows on the doors to see if any stewards were about. The coast looked clear. And then he spotted the table of a small family. More importantly, he discovered the young, beautiful girl seated there. He studied the dynamics. There was some tension, he thought. The girl was pouting, and her parents were ignoring her. Eventually, the young girl stood up, crossed the room, and positioned herself at one of the portholes looking out into the gray Atlantic.

Seeing the adults deep in conversation, Paolo headed toward her to make his move. "Not very pretty, is it?" he asked.

The young woman jumped. "Don't do that," she said.

"Do what?"

"You scared me."

"Oh, I don't think you're easily scared," Paolo teased. "My name's Paolo."

"And you think I'm a pushover for a man—or boy—in uniform," she said.

"Ouch. That hurts," Paolo said, feigning offense. "Don't be fooled by this youthful face. I'm older than you think."

"So that means you're seventeen … because I think you're sixteen," she countered. "I'm Luisa. Luisa Morosco. Those people over there have kidnapped me and are taking me to live in L'America, in a terrible city called New York."

"Oh, but you are mistaken, Luisa. In New York there are many opportunities, especially for someone as bright and outgoing as you," he said.

"And what else, Paolo?" she asked.

"What else?" he repeated.

"Bright, outgoing, and …?" She was flirting.

"Oh, that. Yes, but of course. And short."

She folded her arms and turned away.

"And pretty," he offered. "You are very pretty."

"I forgive you," she said, turning back to him. "Tell me something, Mr. Paolo. Are there any benefits to personally knowing a steward on board?"

"Most certainly," he said with a smile.

"Then you shall have to show me, I'm sure," she said, smiling back.

"Show you what?" her father asked sternly, suddenly appearing beside them.

"The dolphins, Papa. The steward told me they always follow the ship. And you can find them on sunny days."

"I hope you don't mind, sir," Paolo said, bowing. "I'm Paolo. I just wanted your daughter to look forward to something other than wind and rain."

Luisa's father looked unsure. "Yes, well, I'm sure you are very good at what you do, but I am also sure that you have no control over the weather. Please don't give her unreasonable expectations. Her disappointments are a problem for me and her mother. It's time to retire, Luisa. Good evening … Paolo." He firmly pulled Luisa toward the door, where her mother was waiting. In an instant the three of them were gone.

Paolo smiled. He was certain this would not be their last encounter.

"So you like the ladies, young man?" a voice called out.

Paolo spun around to see the officer he had met the first day in steerage.

"I thought so. Where have you been?"

"Ah, all over. I've been … busy," Paolo stammered.

"Well, good. That's what we expect of our stewards. But now that I see you here pining for your little girl, I think I shall introduce you to one of our privileges. Follow me. And hold onto your hat. We'll be outside before we are inside again," he instructed. He turned and exited the dining room.

Paolo hurried to catch up to him. He felt he had no choice.

They descended the stairs to the open deck and ran along the wall, attempting to avoid the wind-driven rain. Paolo was curious when the officer opened the hatch to steerage.

"Don't be a little girl yourself," the officer said. "Sometimes you have to go through shit to find the truffle. You understand Calabrese?"

"No, not really."

"*E rhe spine, nescia la rosa*. In the middle of thorns, the rose blooms," the officer recited. They climbed through the hatch and closed it behind them. As they reached the bottom of the stairs, Paolo was alert. Though his hair was tucked away, he certainly did not want to be recognized by anyone here. There were three areas with makeshift divisions. The first section was assigned to single men. The second was for families, and the third was for women traveling alone. After forcing their way through the first two sections, Paolo and the officer found themselves at the so-called entrance to the last area. Paolo frowned.

"We are in uniform. We may go anywhere on this ship, little man," the officer said. He slid back the tattered curtain to the sounds of screams as dozens of women scurried to protect themselves. A few grabbed at blankets and clothing to cover any exposed skin. The rest sat or stood in various states of undress with blank stares. They had forsaken modesty days ago. The officer followed a predetermined route. "My name is Claudio, by the way. Here in this slum, we use first names," he said.

"Why are we here?" Paolo asked.

"Ah, that you will see soon enough." He fumbled through his jacket pocket and produced a wrinkled piece of paper. He studied it briefly. "Berth 33. Do you see it? Oh yes, right down here." They turned a corner and approached a young lady no more than twenty years old. She was sitting on her mattress but stood immediately upon seeing them.

"Luciana. Am I right?" Claudio asked.

"Yes, sir," she responded quietly.

Several of the women around them laughed and whispered.

The girl appeared nervous. She was pale-skinned with dark eyes and thin lips. She wore a stained chemise through which a pink corset could be seen. Below it, a billowing white slip hung to the middle of her calf. Paolo noticed an odd contrast between the delicate undergarments and her bare feet, which were heavily soiled.

"This is very good," Claudio exclaimed. "Very good indeed. Let's have a look then, girl."

Luciana slid down her corset to reveal her youthful breasts. Paolo turned away instinctively.

"Oh, come now, little man. I'm sure you've seen nature's bounty before. Sit here with me, Luciana." Claudio and the young woman sat on the edge of the berth. He took her hands and studied them carefully. "Your nails are clean. I like that. But your hands are so cold." He suddenly plunged one of them into his pants. "Here, warm them."

Paolo wanted to offer some sort of protection, but Luciana seemed curiously indifferent. She stared forward, not making eye contact with either of them.

"You may remove your hand now, girl," Claudio instructed. "We are ready for a deeper relationship. You understand?"

She nodded, slid her hand back out, and began to unbutton his jacket.

Claudio grabbed her hand. "No, no, no, that takes too much time, and I am a very busy man." He moved her away, drew his legs up onto the mattress, and began to unbuckle his belt. "Come, board Claudio's train," he said, motioning to her. She straddled him and raised her slip. Claudio winked at Paolo and closed the drape that hung from the berth. From inside he called, "Paolo, you will stand guard. Luciana and I require privacy." He laughed loud.

Paolo could hear them behind the curtain. It was more than a little uncomfortable. The women who had been watching now pointed and laughed. Paolo was certainly familiar with the seedier side of life, but this he had not expected. And he felt as though his continued presence was a sign of approval or, worse, partnership. On the other hand, he had to protect his passage on this ship. He had to endure this assignment. So he remained at his post, staring at the floor to avoid the eyes of their audience.

"So I will have work in L'America?" he heard Luciana ask.

"It will be as I have said," Claudio responded. "Signore Fabbiano is in first class, awaiting my list. Rest assured, you are on it. He will seek you out before we arrive. All the arrangements will be made. You will have work indeed."

Claudio opened the drape and stood next to the berth. Luciana sat impassively. Paolo found himself staring at her. When she raised her eyes to him, he quickly looked away.

"Now it is your turn, signore," she said unexpectedly.

Paolo immediately shook his head. "No, no," he said. "I … I must return topside" was all he could manage to say.

"Nonsense, Paolo. You must have a go," Claudio said.

Paolo looked at him. There was an awkward pause. Then finally, he said, "I cannot, Claudio. You must not ask me again. It is a … personal matter." He was emphatic.

Claudio smiled. "Of course, little man. I understand. A personal matter." He turned one last time to look at Luciana, who seemingly could not take her eyes off Paolo. "She likes you. Too bad," Claudio said. The two then pushed their way through the horde of women who pretended to be unaware. "Come, I will introduce you to Signore Fabbiano. This is your lucky day."

CHAPTER 10

"They are coming in such numbers and we are unable adequately
to take care of them … It simply amounts to unrestricted
and indiscriminate dumping into this country of people of
every character and description … If there were in existence a
ship that could hold three million human beings, then three
million Jews of Poland would board to escape to America."
—Congressional hearing, 1920

Anna, please, you must eat something," Aldo pleaded. "It is not good
for the baby."

"The food is not good for the baby," Anna countered. "And I am too
uncomfortable to eat anything. It is so cold in here, Aldo. This is more of

a sheet than a blanket," she said as she adjusted herself under several layers of clothes.

"Do you need more?" Aldo asked. "Salvatore, give me your jacket."

"No. He looks so nice. And he must be cold as well."

"Mama, I am not cold. It is not cold. Take it," Salvatore insisted. He handed the jacket to Aldo, who placed it across Anna's shoulders.

She shivered.

"Anna, I am concerned about you." Aldo touched her forehead. "You may have fever. I'm going for a steward."

Anna grabbed his arm to restrain him. "You'll do no such thing. I'm simply a little cold. You stay with me. Besides, Aldo, the ship's doctors have not done their inspection in a while. I'm sure they will be by soon. Stay."

"Oh yes, the famous ship's doctors. They line us up like cattle, peel back our eyelids, poke us, and check our teeth. I am confident they will make you better," he sneered.

"When you pay for tin, you don't get silver," she mumbled.

"Anna, please ... I tried. There are no cabins left. This is my fault," he moaned.

"It is not your fault. I'm sorry. I'm just tired. I know I have been difficult about this journey. I don't want to go—you know that. But you are doing what you think is right. And I'm making it harder on you. Is there any water?" she asked.

Aldo reached under her berth and removed a small jar. He looked around to be sure no one was watching and then lifted it to her lips. She struggled for a sip.

"Quickly, Anna. If a steward sees the water, he will take it from us.

We are not permitted to bring it from the washroom. Another sorry rule. They think we will use it for cooking. Cooking what? The ship's blankets?"

Just then, a crowd of passengers surged toward the hatch. Quickly, there was chatter all around about an opening and fresh air and the deck. Over it all, loud shouts could be heard, but none of it was understandable. Gradually, the talk around them died down, and the louder voices in the distance clearly belonged to persons in authority. Aldo and Anna looked at each other. This was what they had been waiting for.

"Stand in a line, next to your berths!" one of the voices shouted. "Wait until the doctors have completed their exams of your entire family. If no marks are made, you may then go about your business."

"Anna, do not step down. The doctor can see you where you are," Aldo said.

"I can get up," Anna argued.

"No!" he shouted. "Stay."

"Papa, am I straight?" Salvatore asked.

"Yes, of course. Why?" Aldo asked.

"I saw the doctor take a boy away because he was not straight," Salvatore answered.

"That is nonsense. They don't do such things," Aldo said.

A steward and one of the doctors approached. Both were in uniform. The doctor had a stethoscope around his neck and a pocketful of wooden tongue depressors. The steward held a clipboard.

The doctor frowned at Anna. "Why does she stay in her berth?" he asked. "Come down, signora," he instructed.

"No!" Aldo said just a bit too loud. "She cannot. She is unsteady. She may have fever."

"I cannot examine her up there," the doctor said. "Signora, please. You must stand here. The steward will help you."

Anna sat up slowly and began to slide her legs toward the edge of the berth. She suddenly screamed and slumped over.

Aldo touched her face. "See? See what you've done? Anna, let's put your legs back up," Aldo said as he reached under her knees. "You're wet. Why are you wet?" he asked, withdrawing his arm. His hand was covered in blood. "*Dio mio*! There is blood! Why is there blood?" he screamed at the doctor.

The doctor was expressionless. He leaned over and whispered something to the steward, who immediately disappeared. "Signore ... your wife is pregnant?" he asked.

"Yes, yes, she is. A few months. What is happening?" Aldo pleaded.

Salvatore cowered behind him, not knowing how to react.

"We will need to take her to the infirmary. A stretcher will be here soon. I must insist you remain calm."

"Anna! Anna!" he screamed.

"Aldo, please. Hold my hand," she said weakly.

He reached for her, saw the blood on his hand, and quickly replaced it with his clean one. He angled away so that she could not see him wiping the blood onto his trousers. "I'm here, *il mio amore*. I will not leave your side," Aldo insisted.

Two stewards appeared, carrying a small stretcher. They cleared away some of the passengers who had gathered and laid the stretcher on the floor.

"Signora, I know this will be uncomfortable, but you must let us move you," the doctor said.

"I will help," Aldo said.

"That you will," the doctor agreed, "by standing aside, signore."

As Aldo backed off, he held tightly to Salvatore's collar. He turned his son away so that he could be shielded from the scene. Anna screamed in pain. There was shuffling and arguing among the stewards. Anna screamed again as they mishandled her, finally depositing her on the stretcher. One leaned over her and wrote on the collar of her dress in white chalk, "AS." Then they raised the stretcher, steadied themselves, and carried her away.

"She will be tended to in the infirmary," the doctor said blankly.

"We will come. My son and I will follow you," Aldo said.

"No. You cannot. There are no visitors allowed there."

"But we are not visitors. That is my wife. That is his mother," Aldo said.

"I said no visitors." The doctor was insistent. He held out his arm to hold Aldo at bay. "And remove the bedclothes. Put them on the floor next to this row," he said, pointing. "Someone will come by to pick them up."

With that, he turned and left quickly. Aldo looked at Salvatore, who studied his father's face for reassurance. But there was only fear and confusion. Aldo searched the faces of the passengers who were watching, hoping someone would help him make sense of this. But each time he made eye contact, the reaction was the same—a sudden turn and then disappearance. He held Salvatore's shirt so tightly that he lost feeling in his hand, but he was not about to let go.

◆

"Papa, I don't hear any more rain. Can we go outside ... please?" Franco asked his father.

"Soon, Franco. Soon. I have a plan. You remember the large pipe you asked me about when we were on deck before the storm?"

"Yes. It had white smoke all around it," Franco responded.

"Steam," said Giuseppe. "It is a steam pipe. There were people sitting against it for warmth. We must get to that pipe before the others. Are you well enough to go with me now?"

"Yes! Yes, let's go to the pipe!"

"Listen to me, Franco. If the storm has truly passed, they will open the hatches soon," he whispered in his ear. "We must be ready. Can you walk with me to the stairs and wait?"

"Of course, Papa. I am not so sick right now. But what about our things?"

"Leave them. They are nothing. We'll just take the blankets."

Giuseppe stood, helped his son down from the berth, and wrapped the gray ship's blanket around the boy's head and shoulders. Franco was unsteady. Giuseppe frowned.

"No, Papa, I can go. Please."

Giuseppe grabbed his own blanket. He took Franco's hand and slowly navigated the masses.

"I don't like the mathematics here," Franco complained.

"What do you mean?" his father asked.

"The *laghetto*. There are many more than one hundred and seven in this cellar," Franco said.

"I'm sorry. I did not know."

"I see the stairs," Franco announced.

"Quiet! We must be the first," Giuseppe scolded.

They pushed through a few more families and found the stairs. Giuseppe helped his son halfway up, and they sat hunched below the hatch. It was colder here. Giuseppe made sure Franco was covered. He pulled his own blanket tighter.

Within minutes, they were discovered near the hatch. Hoping this boy and his father knew something, a crowd rushed the stairs. There was pushing and shoving as many fought for position. Giuseppe smiled slightly. He had made the right decision. He thought of the garden and of Marianna. The smile disappeared. He held his son tight and fought the urge to weep.

———————◆———————

"It looks like we may have broken through the storm," Claudio said as he and Paolo made their way along the deck. "If that is the case, we will have to release the animals soon. This deck will be just as vile as steerage. Have you been to first class yet?"

"No, I haven't," Paolo answered, still reeling from the recent events.

"You're in for a treat, little man."

Paolo hated the way Claudio called him that. In fact, Paolo now hated everything about him.

They ascended a staircase unlike the others on the ship. It was wrought iron, with dark wooden trim. The center of each step was decorated with insets of marble and colored stone. Claudio pushed open a two-meter-wide beautiful wooden door. The attendant just inside nodded, and Claudio and Paolo entered. Paolo stopped dead in his tracks.

The huge first-class dining room was two stories tall. The lights and colors nearly blinded him. When his eyes adjusted, he saw walls finished with white and gilt carved-mahogany panels. Magnificent

Corinthian-decorated columns supported a second floor. Every centimeter of the room seemed inlaid with some sort of treasure. A jade-green carpet exploded with a yellow floral pattern.

At the center of it all, rising high above the floor, was a round conical ceiling with large stained glass windows, each depicting a different historical event. Paolo had never seen anything so ornate outside of a cathedral. He didn't count, but he was certain there were more white-gloved attendants than passengers.

"Well, move along, little man," Claudio said impatiently. "We have business here."

Claudio ushered Paolo through the dining hall toward the far corner. They approached a door bordered by large panels of etched glass. It was difficult to see inside, but Paolo made out the figure of a man sitting alone at a small table. Claudio knocked on the door, and an attendant opened it. The man inside motioned to allow them entrance.

The room was small, decorated with mahogany writing desks, circular tables, and red furnishings. A large humidor covered one wall, and each table had a crystal ashtray and an ornate silver lighter. The man sat alone, smoking a thick cigar. His left hand embraced a partially filled brandy snifter. An impressive-looking bottle sat nearby.

"Leave us," he instructed the attendant, who vacated the room, closing the door behind him. "Come, sit, Claudio. Introduce me to your friend," the man said.

They quickly sat at the remaining two chairs at the table. The man, in his forties, wore a white suit, with a handsome waistcoat and a blue and gold silk tie. He wasn't particularly large, but he somehow gave the impression that he was. He carefully dipped the unlit end of the cigar into the brandy, twirled it, and placed it to his lips. A blue haze surrounded his round face and temporarily obscured pockmarks and uneven skin.

"This is Paolo, Signore Fabbiano. He is new to our ship," Claudio said.

Fabbiano cocked his head to one side and studied Paolo. "And why should we be talking with Paolo?"

"I think he can be useful to us. He is very resourceful," Claudio said.

"How so?" Fabbiano questioned.

"Well, he managed to board the ship in Palermo and pretend to be a steward all this time," Claudio announced.

Paolo shook. His surprise was obvious.

"Oh, come now, little man. Did you really think I didn't know?" Claudio asked.

Paolo was speechless. He worried what their next move would be. Was this gentleman an enforcer or perhaps the ship's owner? What would happen when they arrived in L'America? Suddenly, his little plan was coming apart at the seams. He had never really considered the consequences.

"Signorino Paolo, you must realize there are very serious penalties for stowaways, especially those who impersonate a ship's steward," Fabbiano said sternly.

Paolo said nothing.

"So what are we going to do with him, Claudio?"

"That depends," Claudio answered.

"On his level of cooperation," Fabbiano concluded. "I understand. Do you understand, Claudio's little man?"

All Paolo could manage to do was shake his head no.

"Then I shall educate you," Fabbiano said. "Claudio and I have certain … interests … on this ship. And it's a very simple arrangement. I need employees in New York City. He provides them. He is paid handsomely for his services here. I am paid handsomely for mine in L'America. The sea aboard our ship is particular crowded with fish this trip, but Claudio has but one net. I don't like leaving food on the table. It's such a waste. But now we have you."

"Wait a minute," Paolo said, finally able to speak. "I don't think I can do what Claudio does."

"The little man can talk," Fabbiano said. "Well, that is a start. And let us be very clear about this whole affair. We are not forcing you to do anything. Right, Claudio? You have choices."

"Choices?" Paolo repeated.

"But of course. There are always choices. Claudio, if you would please, explain the choices to your little man," Fabbiano said.

"Certainly. On the one hand, Paolo, you can cooperate with us— perform some duties while on board, be my assistant, so to speak," Claudio explained. "For that, your masquerade will be safe with us, even protected. On the other hand, if you do not wish to work with us, I will be forced to fulfill my sworn duty and turn you over to the ship's authorities. They will take you into custody. You will not be allowed off this ship until we return to Palermo. There you will be tried, found guilty, and sent to prison for five to ten years."

"If I become your … assistant … what happens when we arrive in L'America?" Paolo asked.

"Ahhh, that is the beauty of your new relationship," Fabbiano answered. "We will provide you with a worry-free transfer in New York. You will be allowed to disembark to a special launch, which will bypass the perils of Ellis Island and take you directly to shore. What's more, I will introduce you to my associates there—very good people to know. You will have my recommendation. I have a feeling your skills could be very helpful to them."

"So you see?" Claudio said. "As I said to you earlier, this is your lucky day."

CHAPTER 11

———

Ed io le dissi: "Addio, Calavresella,
Na veppeta de st'acqua name darria,"
Calavresella acconcia e bella,
Calavresella, Calavrese.

I said to her, "Hello, Calabrian Maiden,
Do not deny me a taste of your water,"
Calabrian Maiden, tanned and fair
Calabrian Maiden, the Calabrian.
—Calabrese folk song

When the sun finally emerged, so did the hundreds of broken passengers in steerage. As the hatches were mercifully opened, they surfaced like ants and immediately covered every meter of deck space. Their ashen faces sought the sun. They filled their lungs with fresh air, breathing deeply in an attempt to replace the foul substance they had been subjected to for more than a week. Some were practically catatonic. Others coughed violently and vomited on themselves. Few were unaffected by the vile dungeon that had imprisoned them since the start of their voyage. Even the Cossacks were less animated.

The deck was blanketed with bodies—hundreds upon hundreds of men, women, and children. Except for the occasional frightened child or protective patriarch, it was eerily quiet. Most were too sick or too exhausted or too despondent. On the other hand, the decks above were lively. The second- and first-class passengers were getting their first open-deck opportunities as well. They were jubilant. Many bent over the railings to study the luckless lot below. Those who weren't snickering and pointing or turning away repulsed felt sorry for their fellow travelers and dropped leftover treats from their abundance into the arms of the most energetic.

In time, stiff extremities began to uncoil, and color returned to the faces of many of those on the lower deck. The sound stirred from breath to murmur to spirit. One fellow even unwrapped a hurdy-gurdy and began playing. The Calabrese within earshot joined in choruses of "La Calavresella."

Sera la viddi, La Calavresella,
Chianno, chianillo da l'aqua veniva,
Calavresella acconcia e bella,
Calavresella, Calavrese.

I saw her this evening, the Calabrian Maiden,
Slowly, slowly from where the water was,
Calabrian Maiden, tanned and fair
Calabrian Maiden, the Calabrian.

Giuseppe Mosca, unaware that he was smiling for the first time since the wagon pulled away from the mud hut, nodded his head in time. Franco smiled as well and mimicked his father's actions. The steam pipe was warm, and the music even warmer. Giuseppe turned his ear to a familiar sound in the distance. He sought it out. As it grew louder, his eyes brightened. Someone was playing a *zampogna*. When he was a child, his evenings often had been filled with the haunting melodies his father had created on the strange-looking instrument. His father would blow on the wooden pipe and squeeze the white canvas bag as his fingers nimbly danced across the open keys. Giuseppe had never tired of those moments when his father would take a breath, but the air in the bag would still support the notes.

> *Ed io le dissi: "Addio, Calavresella,*
> *Na veppeta de st'acqua name darria,"*
> *Calavresella acconcia e bella,*
> *Calavresella, Calavrese.*

> I said to her, "Hello, Calabrian Maiden,
> Do not deny me a taste of your water,"
> Calabrian Maiden, tanned and fair
> Calabrian Maiden, the Calabrian.

The music was a balm to the topside emigrants, now refugees from both homeland and berth. Throughout the deck, baskets and boxes were thrown open as the passengers eagerly dug into their stores of cheese and bread and wine. Stale crusts and moldy outer layers of provolone and pecorino did nothing to dampen their spirits. There was laughter—and not just the barbaric snorts of the Serbs, who routinely laughed at their own disgusting behavior. It was a merriment that had been absent for the entire voyage.

> *Ed essa me respunne, garbata e bella,*
> *"Non sulo l'acqua, la perzona mia,"*
> *Calavresella accocia e bella,*
> *Calavresella, Calavrese.*

> And she answered, that gentle and beautiful maiden,
> "Not only the water, but also myself,"
> Calabrian Maiden, tanned and fair
> Calabrian Maiden, the Calabrian.

Aldo Grimaldi had no interest in hurdy-gurdies and *zampognas*. Holding fast to Salvatore's jacket sleeve, he snaked his way through the multitude in search of Anna, or at least someone who had information about her. "Where is the infirmary?" he asked a wrinkled woman.

But the woman just continued clapping gaily to the music.

"Stop for a moment, please. Do you know where the infirmary is?"

She shook her head and turned away from him, as though his distress might threaten her mood.

Over and over again, Aldo asked the same question. And over and over again, from those who didn't ignore him, he got the same response. For more than an hour, he desperately sought anyone who could direct him to his ailing wife. Salvatore said nothing throughout the ordeal. He was worried about his mother, but he was scared for his father. Aldo was a man who had always exhibited a steady hand. He rarely raised his voice, even when disciplining Salvatore. His calm demeanor had been a constant source of comfort to the boy. Aldo's anxiety was not only unfamiliar; it was terrifying.

Finally, Aldo spied two stewards leaning against the bow.... One, young and classically handsome with longish hair. The other at least fifteen years his elder was tall and gangly. Surely, stewards would have knowledge of Anna's location. With Salvatore in tow, he pushed his way through the ten meters of bodies that separated him from the two men.

"Signori, please ... signori, where can I find the infirmary?" he asked.

The older steward, who wore an officer's stripes on his shoulder, was clearly annoyed at the interruption. "Can you not see that we are talking?" he asked.

"Yes, yes, I see, but please ... I must find my wife."

"She's in the infirmary?" the officer asked.

"Yes," Aldo answered.

"Then you have found her, signore. Now leave us," the man said.

"No, you don't understand. I don't know where the infirmary is," Aldo said.

"The location of the infirmary is of no use to you. You cannot go there. You cannot be there. It has no visiting hours. Where are you from?"

"Naples," Aldo replied.

"Well then," the officer snapped, "I suggest you make your way back to Ospedali Riunity and see the attendant at the front desk. She will direct you to anyone you would like to see there. They have visiting hours. We do not. Have I made myself clear?"

The younger steward said nothing but looked uncomfortable.

"Yes, yes, I understand," Aldo pleaded. "But she was taken more than a week ago. There must be some word."

"And you will receive it when we arrive in L'America." The officer was now clearly angry. "Go, before I remove you myself and confine you and your street urchin to the steerage barnyard you came from."

Aldo pulled Salvatore closer and backed away. He had fire in his chest, but he was not going to put Salvatore in harm's way. He hated his decision. He hated this ship. And he hated the godforsaken music that these ignorant peasants were squawking.

———————◆———————

Hours later, Aldo and Salvatore were still roaming the deck, this time without a sense of purpose. Sporadically, Salvatore caught his father mumbling to himself. After a while, it unnerved him so much that he leaned in to try to hear his whispers. At first, he caught nothing but half words and nonsense. Eventually, he understood. His father was praying.

"*Piacere a Dio. Vi prego. Salvare mia moglie. Mi perdoni i miei peccati. Piacere a Dio. Vi prego. Salvare mia moglie. Mi perdoni i miei peccati. Piacere a Dio. Vi prego. Salvare mia moglie. Mi perdoni i miei peccati.* Please, God. I beg you. Save my wife. Forgive me my sins." Over and over again.

At first Aldo didn't notice the young steward standing behind him. But Salvatore did. Salvatore tugged at his father's coat, but he was ignored. He tugged again. Still nothing. Aldo was deep in his repetitive prayer.

"Signore," the steward said. "Signore, a minute please."

Aldo eventually turned and recognized the young man who had stood alongside the rude steward an hour earlier. "So the young man wants to threaten me as well?" Aldo asked.

"No, signore. Please, I want to help. Claudio doesn't understand," the young man explained.

"And you do? You understand?"

The young steward was silent. He wanted this man to know that he was a comrade—that he shared his pain, that he was more kin than foe. "More than you think, signore." The steward looked around. "Please, signore, we must be discreet."

"You are hiding from your friend?" Aldo asked.

"He is not my friend. Quickly, what is your name?" the young man asked.

"Aldo … Aldo Grimaldi."

"And your wife?"

"Anna. Anna Grimaldi."

"Stay in this area. I will inquire at the infirmary and meet you back here," the steward instructed.

"But why?" Aldo asked. "Why would you do this?"

"I will be back shortly," the steward said, and he hurried away.

"Papa?" Salvatore questioned. "Will he bring Mama to us?"

"I don't know, my son. I don't know."

———————◆———————

Paolo ascended the stairs that led to second class. The infirmary was little more than a storage room crammed with narrow cots, dented cabinets, and IV bottles suspended from makeshift poles. It smelled of alcohol and urine. The staff was ill-equipped to handle the load and wore stained smocks and scowls. Paolo was determined to locate Anna Grimaldi and depart as quickly as possible.

"Can I help you?" a man with a large facial scar that extended from just below his left eye to the base of his ear lobe asked. "I'm Doctor Falasca. And we have no more room."

"No, I don't have a patient. I'm looking for one," Paolo said.

"Take your pick. We have many," Falasca quipped.

"Her name is Grimaldi. Anna Grimaldi."

"Grimaldi ... Grimaldi," the doctor said, pondering. "Oh, yes ... Grimaldi. *Aborto spontaneo.*"

"She had a miscarriage?" Paolo asked.

"Yes. And what concern is it of yours?" Falasca asked.

"I know the family. I want to get them word."

"She will be fine. They'll be reunited with her when we reach L'America. Anything else?"

"No, no. She's …?"

"Fine. Now as you can see, we have much work to do here. You found your way in. You can find your way out," the doctor said, walking away.

Paolo quickly made his way back down to the deck, heading for the area where he had instructed Aldo Grimaldi to wait. Suddenly, a firm hand gripped his shoulder, and he turned to find Claudio leering at him. At first he said nothing. Since Claudio seemed to have eyes in the back of his head, Paolo assumed he knew where Paolo had been.

"Claudio, I just wanted to help," he managed to say.

"Is that not precisely what you are expected to do? Help me and Signore Fabbiano?"

"Yes, but …"

"Where are the names and berths?" Claudio asked.

"I have them," Paolo answered.

"Well?" Claudio held out his hand.

Paolo reached into his jacket pocket and produced a wrinkled paper. "Here. Just as you asked," he said as he handed it over.

Claudio studied the paper. "Six … you have six names," he said.

"Yes. It was my first time."

"Six. And if I go and see them, will they comply?" Claudio asked.

"They expect you," Paolo said blankly.

"Will they comply?" Claudio repeated, suddenly shouting.

"Yes. They want work. They will … comply."

"We will see. Your uncomplicated arrival in L'America depends upon it. Get me more. Six is very disappointing for an attractive young man such as you. In two days we land. See to it that my pockets are full. Understand?" Claudio asked.

"I understand," Paolo replied.

"And forget your friends from Naples. You have work to do. Besides, they have been returned to steerage. Go," Claudio instructed.

———◆———

Paolo's gait was suddenly heavy and labored. For the first time in a very long while, he felt conflicted. In Palermo, survival had necessitated not just cheeky confidence and talented hands but a hardened heart as well. Considering the plight of his victims would have meant death to his trade. So he had made it a game and disregarded both their circumstances and their faces. He had known that if he regarded them as nothing more than supply, he could manipulate them without remorse.

This was different. He found himself coercing women barely out of their teens into the service of the likes of Claudio and Fabbiano. But at the same time, he needed safe passage from this ship. And he needed L'America. So a handful of girls were added to the streets of New York. He was probably doing them a favor. After all, they would have work, a place to live, and food to eat. This was best for all concerned.

So why did he feel sick as he solicited another fourteen girls over the next two days? Fourteen. Who was Claudio kidding? He couldn't possibly "test" fourteen more before they landed.

———◆———

Franco noticed it first—calmer waters, the cry of gulls. Those who had made the trip before changed their clothes and furiously packed their belongings. Seeing this, Giuseppe instructed Franco to do the same and then pushed him along an aisle and up the stairway until they were back on the deck. Everyone, it seemed, who was traveling from Palermo and Naples now jostled for a glimpse of land.

The morning was full of mist, and droplets formed on the shoulders of the thousands who now gathered along the railings. Ferry boats passed in and out of the fog, and other giant sea beasts emitted their own guttural sounds as they vied for position. To the right, green stretches of Long Island emerged. To the left, the shoreline came into view. Ultimately, the mist could not obscure the mighty city directly ahead of them.

Suddenly, the lady of the harbor appeared before them. Tall and green, the regal statue silently announced their arrival, captivating everyone on board. Children saluted as a gun sounded from Governors Island. Her shadow enveloped the *Santa Ana*. Many of the travelers instinctively crossed themselves and then raised their hands, symbolically touching her robe in what felt like their first contact with L'America. "La Madonna!" they chanted. "La Madonna!"

CHAPTER 12

Give me your tired, your poor,
Your huddled masses yearning to breathe free,
The wretched refuse of your teeming shore,
Send these, the homeless, tempest-tost, to me,
I lift my lamp beside the golden door.
—Emma Lazarus, "The New Colossus"

Anchors exploded from the hull as the great chains drove them down into the black water, eventually burying them into the silt of New York Harbor. The gangplanks were spun around and dropped onto the dock, but those in steerage were held back by a line of stewards. First- and second-class passengers were waved on. It wasn't until the last of the upper classes had received a very superficial examination by immigration officials who had boarded earlier and all had disembarked that the uniformed crew allowed steerage to move forward.

The temporary railings that had directed the privileged to the interior of the main building were now repositioned. Franco pressed against Giuseppe. "Why do they change the fence?" he asked.

"I don't know. Stay close. I don't know," Giuseppe answered.

Finally, a metal gate swung open, and the hundreds on deck were funneled toward the narrow makeshift walkway. Eventually, Giuseppe and Franco made their way to the top of the gangplank. Before allowing them to pass through, stewards lifted the cards that had been pinned to their hats. They displayed two handwritten figures that coincided with the manifest page and line number where their names had been recorded at the start of their journey.

After checking the clipboard, the steward nodded, and the two proceeded down the gangplank. When they reached the bottom, however, they were surprised that the railings actually turned them away from the buildings. After about fifteen minutes, the end of the line came into view. Giuseppe's heart sank. The railings turned back to the edge of the dock, where an open-air ferry was filling up with the passengers ahead of them.

A scuffle was developing about twenty meters in front of them. The wooden railing shook as an elderly man and his wife refused to board the vessel. They clung to the ropes for dear life. "No! No! We are not going back. You cannot send us back!" the red-faced man shouted. His wife seemingly didn't know whether to protest with him or protect him.

Finally, an officer in charge approached them and pulled the couple aside. Giuseppe could not hear the conversation, but the couple reluctantly rejoined the line and boarded.

"The poor old man doesn't understand," someone whispered to Giuseppe.

Giuseppe turned and looked at the man in confusion.

"The boat. It takes us to the island … the Ellis Island. Over there." He pointed. "They check your papers, your health, your money. Then you can come back. You will come back."

Giuseppe was unsure. He didn't trust the stranger with the crooked smile. He thought he was up to something, but Giuseppe had no choice but to move forward. He and Franco boarded the strange-looking boat.

———◆———

The *Santa Ana* was still depositing its human cargo back on the dock in Lower Manhattan as Claudio and Signore Fabbiano gave Paolo his last-minute instructions. They had ushered him safely off the ship, as promised. Paolo was mesmerized by the size of everything—the buildings, the crowds, the piers.

"Take Signore Fabbiano's valise, little man," Claudio said. He handed the leather bag to Paolo, along with a piece of paper. "You will escort him to a shop on Cuyler's Alley. The address is on the paper. There you will receive further instructions. You will listen. You must not talk. And stop looking around. A student who watches the flowers outside the window is a student who fails the examination."

Paolo found his proverbs irritating.

Claudio stood aside with Fabbiano for a moment. They laughed and exchanged good-byes.

"All right, Signore Paolo, let's be off," Fabbiano instructed. "I cannot wait to take a proper bath and eat food prepared for one." With that, he guided Paolo away, and Claudio ran ahead to join those boarding the ferry.

———◆———

Aldo and Salvatore Grimaldi were near the front of the ferry. There was no escaping the incessant cold spray that doused them all the way from the dock to Ellis Island. Aldo was worried about the baggage. He was worried about the examinations and questions he had been told to expect. But mostly he worried about Anna. How would he find her? Did they transport the sick to this place called Ellis? Was she out of the cold?

"Papa, you see?" Salvatore asked. He pointed to the red and white buildings that seemed to rise out of the water. "How do they float?"

"It is an island," Aldo explained.

"Is that Isola delle Lacrime?" Salvatore asked.

"Who called it that?" Aldo questioned.

"A man in the line said we were going to the Island of Tears. I will not cry there, Papa. I am too old to cry."

"On this trip, you have become a man, Salvatore. A man." Aldo watched as the buildings grew larger and larger. He had not expected so many. Some looked to be four and five stories, and except for a large grassy area that separated two long rows of military-looking structures, the entire island was covered with them.

This small city in the middle of the harbor was nearly split in two by a very wide body of water—apparently, where the ferry was headed. *Twenty minutes*, Aldo thought. Twenty minutes was all the time they had been allowed on the mainland of L'America before being shuttled off to some remote island of concrete that, at least from this vantage point, seemed vacant of any personality.

The ferry lurched as it slowed upon entering the channel in the middle of the island. Salvatore fell into a scowling old man. The man glared at the boy, his face covered in brown wrinkles and uneven stubble. "Look out for the button-hook men, little boy," the old man hissed.

"I beg your pardon?" Aldo asked. "It was an accident. No need to scare my son."

"All the same, both of you will be facing the button-hook men soon enough," he snarled.

"The what?" Aldo asked.

The man laughed and disappeared into the crowd.

"What men is he talking about, Papa? I didn't like him."

"It's nothing, I'm sure," Aldo reassured his son. "This trip has been hard on everyone, especially the older ones."

In an area near the front of the ferry, about twenty young women had gathered. A steward was questioning them, and there was much arguing.

Claudio approached and interrupted. "No, no, signore, I have them. I have their papers. They have husbands waiting inside the Great Hall. Come now, ladies, no sad faces. It is your wedding day!" Claudio pointed to the approaching island of buildings. "Look. Look how beautiful. The start of your new life in L'America!"

When the ferry docked at Ellis Island, hundreds upon hundreds surged toward the gangplank, but the stewards were having none of it. Apparently, thirteen days at sea had tried everyone's patience. Passengers were pushed and shoved, and the smaller ones, especially the children, were knocked carelessly about.

"Franco, please hold onto my leg, damn you!" Giuseppe screamed. "Do you want to get lost? You want to be lost in L'America?"

"Papa, I can't see you!" Franco implored.

"You have my leg. You can see me once we are off this godforsaken boat!"

The scene was repeated over and over again as a thousand emigrants jockeyed for position in what must have felt like their last chance to put down on dry land. Confusion abounded. Tempers flared. Epithets in what seemed like a hundred different languages filled the air, which was already thick with rotting food and body odor.

When the gate was opened to allow the first of the steerage passengers off the ferry, the rush of bodies was more than the uniformed crew could manage. More than a dozen fell forward, only to be trampled by those who followed. The gate was slammed closed, and the crowd pushed back.

"All right!" an officer shouted. "All right! If you animals want to kill each other, wait until you get to Mulberry Street, where it'll be on someone else's time. I'm not cleaning up wop blood or whatever the hell else kinda blood you got running through your foul-smelling skin. So you will settle down, or we will wait!"

The crew held them back a moment while translations were exchanged and the injured were helped away. Again the gate was opened, and this time the passengers were a bit more disciplined. Fortunately, Giuseppe and Franco were far enough back to avoid the danger. And in time, they were able to disembark and follow the long line that stretched from the dock into the baggage room of the main building, finally winding up a steep flight of stairs to the second floor. All the while, men and women in uniform barked unintelligible orders and pointed fingers.

They were three abreast as they made their way up and into the Great Hall of the registry room. Unbeknownst to most, the inspection process had already begun as doctors scanned the line for limps and shuffles, coughs and wheezes. Every once in a while, a child was asked his or her name to ensure that the child was not deaf or dumb. And if a child as young as two years old was in the arms of a parent, he or she was taken and made to walk.

The initial examination itself was rather quick. The intent was to check for a list of more than sixty symptoms, but time did not permit this. Since they processed thousands of people a day, the doctors were rather skilled at superficial diagnoses. They looked for scalp and nail fungi, varicose veins, signs of epilepsy, and tuberculosis. Every once in a while, an examiner would write in chalk on a person's lapel or outerwear—L for lameness, G for goiter, S for senility, and a host of other marks that went unexplained to the frightened passenger. These individuals were detained for further examination.

Aldo and Salvatore moved through the process without incident until the two were motioned to a small containment area just outside the maze. Here, some sort of facial inspection was being performed, but exactly what kind of exam was unclear until they reached the front.

"Next," a doctor instructed.

Aldo looked at his son and hesitated.

"No, no, the two of you together. Right here. Quickly."

They approached the stern physician, who motioned them closer.

"You first, signore," he said to Aldo. "Look up."

Aldo raised his face as the doctor produced a button hook from his jacket pocket. The doctor used the instrument to turn Aldo's eyelids inside out, first one and then the other, to look for inflammation inside. Aldo tried to shield Salvatore from seeing how much this hurt, but the pain seared through the thin skin of each lid, causing him to flinch and moan.

"Sir, you must be still," the doctor warned.

The experience was over in seconds but seemed interminable. By the time Aldo looked around, Salvatore was already undergoing the agonizing exam. He screeched and fought as an assistant held him down. All Aldo could do was stand by and pray that it would end soon. Eventually, it did, and the two were cleared to move on.

"Papa," Salvatore wailed, "I said I would not cry, but it hurt so bad."

"I know, my son," Aldo said, holding him. "I think I cried a little too."

"Why do they do that?" Salvatore asked.

"*Il tracoma*," Aldo answered. "It's a very bad eye disease. But we are fine. We do not have *il tracoma*. I think we can stay in L'America now. Soon we will find Mama, *se il Signore e disposto*. If the Lord is willing. Soon."

———————◆———————

The Great Hall was a chaotic symphony of groans and wails and incomprehension. Passengers were herded like cattle and prodded along by uniformed officials whose instructions were met with either blank stares or appeals in odd dialects. Dewitt Jennings and Roy Simpson, two such officials, had been through days such as this a thousand times. And a thousand days had done little to diminish their exasperation.

For Dewitt, it was the noise. His left ear had been damaged in an apartment collapse a number of years ago, so the right one did all the work. The pandemonium of the Great Hall assaulted him in waves. By the end of the day, his patience was exhausted. Roy was surly and ill-tempered. He hated the idea that his job was to facilitate the arrival of thousands and thousands of dirty foreigners who seemed to fill every square inch of his city with their grease and the smell of garlic.

"C'mon, ya damn Dagos, move your asses toward the front of the line. Yeah, you … who do ya think I'm talkin' to?" Roy spit.

An elderly man and woman looked at him blankly.

"You! You! That's right, y-o-u. Learn the language or go back home."

"Keep it down, Roy. Nelson's around somewhere. You'll get written up," Dewitt warned.

"Look at that one, Jennings. He's got some kinda white crap all over his lips, like he kissed some powder or something," Roy said, pointing. "You think we should tell one of the docs?"

"The hell with them. Then you gotta fill out a form. He must've seen a doctor. Let it go," Dewitt said.

"We're like a damn welcoming committee for their measles, diphtheria, favus—you name it," Roy complained.

"That's why they got all them hospitals here—eighteen wards of these people with contagious crap. They got it covered," Dewitt said.

"Yeah, yeah, yeah, you can't tell me that when these guineas leave here, they ain't dumpin' all their infections at the foot of Sixteenth Street. That's all I'm sayin'."

"I ain't so much worried about them things as I am about the new Psychopathic Pavilion they got goin' now," Dewitt said. "You see the size of that place? The docs say it's for idiots, imbeciles, and epileptics. I see Italians, Slavs, and Jews checkin' outta that building every day. Them are the new neighbors I'm frettin' about."

———◆———

Claudio and his band of young women were ushered into a small room to the side of the Great Hall and were made to sit in what resembled pews. At the far end was a raised bench with four high-back chairs. From behind, a door swung open, and a judge appeared in a black robe. Claudio started to nudge the girls to their feet.

"No, no. No formalities here," the judge said, waving them back down. "So where are your fiancés, ladies? Not being left at the altar, are we? Claudio?" He seemed impatient.

"They come now, your honor," Claudio said.

From the back, there was some commotion, and as the double doors opened, about twenty young men hurried into the room. They appeared confused.

"Here we are, your honor, the eager husbands," Claudio pronounced. "Come, gentlemen. The judge is a busy man. Find your bride and bring her forward."

The men looked about, not sure of how to proceed.

"Here, here," Claudio insisted. "Take her. And you, take her. And so on." He pulled the men toward the women and matched them up indiscriminately. "That's it. There you go." In short order they were all paired up and standing before the judge.

"So gentlemen, do you take these women to be your wives?" the judge asked.

There was silence. Claudio moved in. "A simple yes, boys. A simple yes. Follow the instructions," Claudio demanded.

The young men responded with a smattering of "I dos."

"Ladies?" the judge asked.

"Sì, sì," Claudio instructed.

Some complied. Others stood mute. Claudio looked to the judge for confirmation. There was an awkward pause.

"By the power vested in me by the state of New York, I now pronounce you husband and wife. You may … do whatever you want to do," the judge said, waving his hand in the direction of the group. "Claudio, if you would be so kind," he continued, motioning for the steward to join him behind the bench.

"Ladies, gentlemen, wait here. We are not finished," Claudio said. He approached the judge. Whispers were exchanged, and the judge handed Claudio a stack of papers. Claudio slid an envelope into the judge's robe. And just that quickly, the judge was gone.

CHAPTER 13

They began life in the new world shunted through chutes from
holding pens to processing stations on the modern model of
efficiently slaughtering livestock …
They believed with all their hearts in the pursuit of happiness,
and had pursued it all the way to this maze of chutes.
—Carmine Sarracino, "Twelve Facts about the Immigrants"

Aldo and Salvatore Grimaldi continued to follow the maze of open
passageways and metal railings as they bent their way toward the main
part of the Ellis Island registry room. The hall was loud and confusing.
Everywhere they looked, the new arrivals were being subjected to bizarre
tests. Some immigrants were being asked to solve simple arithmetic
problems. Others were counting backward. Still others were given puzzles

or geometric shapes to duplicate. All of this was occurring in the midst of so many languages crying out simultaneously.

Eventually, they arrived at the far end of the hall, where legal inspectors wearing starched collars and serge jackets—wool, four-button coats with large pockets—stood alongside translators fluent in many languages and dialects. The inspectors verified information that appeared on the manifest sheet and cross-referenced the manifest numbers with those on the cards that were still pinned to their hats.

The inspectors wanted to know each immigrant's family name, given name, age, sex, occupation, place of origin, nearest relative in country of origin, final destination, money in possession, condition of health, possible status as polygamist or anarchist, complexion, and on and on and on. On either side of Aldo, as far as the eye could see, the scene was being repeated.

Standing next to Salvatore was a boy who also was accompanying what appeared to be his father. They exchanged cautious smiles as their fathers were drilled with question after question. Salvatore reached into his pocket and removed a small Tinkertoy he had played with throughout the trip. The other boy reached into his pocket to reveal a wooden soldier. They laughed. And then the boy held out his toy, offering it to Salvatore. Salvatore looked at it and then considered his own. Instinctively, the two exchanged their toys.

The boy's father tugged on his son's sleeve. "Come. We are finally done here, Franco … come," he said.

Salvatore Grimaldi waved good-bye. The boy called Franco waved back as his father led him away.

"Signore Grimaldi," one of the translators called out. "You are meeting family?"

"Yes … Roberto Micheli. He is my uncle," Aldo answered.

"Michaels," the translator said. "Bob Michaels."

"*Che e* Bob Michaels? Who is Bob Michaels?" Aldo questioned.

"It says here that he is your uncle, from Cleveland."

"Sì, sì, Kellisland. They have some big water there. And stones to cut," Aldo said.

"Your aunt and uncle are waiting outside," the translator explained.

"But signore … my wife," Aldo began to plead.

"We know about your wife. Go find your family. They have arranged passage for you to Cleveland. You will proceed down the stairs on the right. They lead to the currency exchange and railway ticket windows. Your family will meet you there."

"Bob Michaels?" Aldo was confused.

"You must go now," the translator insisted.

Aldo and his son gathered their things and proceeded down the stairs. The further down they moved, the louder the noise grew. When they reached the bottom, it seemed to Aldo that all of L'America was there to welcome the immigrants. Scores waved signs and called out names in every conceivable language. Aldo worried that locating Zio Roberto would be impossible. He grabbed Salvatore tighter and decided the best course would be to elbow his way through the throng, shouting, "Micheli! Micheli!" Salvatore joined in, turning it into a bit of a game.

After nearly an hour, Aldo was exhausted, hoarse, and despondent. He instructed Salvatore to put down the bags he was carrying. Aldo placed his boxes alongside, and the two sat on them. All around, reunions were exploding, and he watched husbands and wives, mothers and sons, brothers and sisters embracing, laughing, crying.

So this was L'America. Perhaps the Giamattis had been right. Naples had survived for centuries. Antonio Salandra and his war and the Camorra presented challenges, to be sure, but according to Raimondo Giamatti, they were not about to take Italy and their beloved city down. Aldo could still see his father-in-law screaming at him for abandoning his sacred heritage and carrying his daughter off to live with philistines and the refuse of Europe.

"Aldo? Aldo?" a woman's voice called out.

At first Aldo thought he was daydreaming. But then it called again. "Aldo!"

This time the familiarity could not be mistaken. He jumped up and turned to see Anna, with Salvatore already clutching his mother's skirt.

"Anna, *il mio amore*! Anna!" he cried as he drew her close to him. "But how?" he asked, and then suddenly, he stood back. "Oh, I'm sorry, my love. I must be more tender. The baby."

In an instant, a flood of tears washed her cheeks as she shook her head and pulled Aldo back to her. "No, Aldo. No. *Aborto spontaneo*. I had a miscarriage. I am so sorry. I am so sorry!"

"No, I am a fool. It was the trip. I did this. I should have listened to your father. Forgive me, *il mio amore*. Can you ever forgive me?" He began to weep.

"Aldo, you must not. The doctor said this was inevitable. He said it would have happened in Naples. You are not to blame. But see, we are together again. Salvatore, we will never be separated again. Never," Anna insisted. "But our family is not so small," she continued. "Look, your uncle comes from the railway window. They all come—Roberto, Teresa, Carlo, and Gianni."

The Micheli family surrounded the Grimaldis with hugs and laughter and kisses. Clean-shaven, with slicked-back salt and pepper hair and casually attired, Roberto was the first to reach them. "We found her for you, Aldo," he announced.

"Welcome to America!" exclaimed Teresa. Dressed in a simple smock, she hurried over from several meters away. "You remember your cousins, Carlo and Gianni."

Carlo, twenty-three, was quite tall and thin. He had a wry smile and an air of maturity beyond his years. His brother Gianni, though only two years younger, was boisterous and boyish. He had a strong, stocky build and seemed ready at any moment for mischief.

"Of course. But they were this high," Aldo said, motioning with his hand on his hip. "The food in L'America must agree with you."

"America," Roberto corrected. "America. We do not say 'L'America' here. You will learn. There is much to learn. But let's get home to Cleveland. We must take the ferry to Jersey City. There we will board a peanut roaster for our trip west."

"Peanut roaster?" Salvatore questioned.

"It is what we call a locomotive here in America—a peanut roaster, a coffee pot," Roberto said.

"Must we eat the peanuts and drink the coffee?" Salvatore asked.

"Of course not, cousin," Gianni replied. "They are just words. And you will learn them too."

With that, they all proceeded to the exits and the ferries.

"But why did you bring the entire family from so far away to meet us? It was not necessary, Uncle," Aldo protested.

"You have traveled thousands of miles, Aldo," Roberto said. "This was the least we could do. Family, eh?" He put his arm around his nephew.

"We must change our lire, no?" Aldo asked, pointing to the sign for currency exchange.

"No, nephew, not here," Roberto said. "The rate here is very bad. We will wait until we get to Cleveland. Our bank there will give us the best exchange rate. Here they are wolves. Carlo, Gianni, why are your hands empty? Help with the bags."

As the young men struggled with the boxes and bags, they pushed each other and laughed but eventually managed to collect everything.

Roberto shook his head. "Yes, they have grown, Aldo, but still they are youngsters. Welcome to America, Grimaldi. Welcome to America."

◆

Signore Fabbiano and Paolo LaChimia headed south on West Street, eventually turning onto Battery Place. They passed Bowling Green, the Produce Exchange at Whitehall and Stone Streets, and Pearl and Water before finally nearing their destination on Cuyler's Alley. Paolo's arms were sore from managing his "employer's" bags. He wondered why a man of his means would insist on walking when he could certainly afford transportation.

The walk itself had been curious. Fabbiano had not spoken a word. And Paolo was not about to initiate any conversation. He walked several paces behind. Fabbiano's attire was impressive even from the back. His blue Cheviot suit fit perfectly. It was accented by a checked, single-breasted waistcoat, a prominent gold watch chain, a wing-collared shirt, a silk bow tie, and a gray Homburg hat. And if it was possible, even his gait seemed stately. Given the horrifying circumstances Paolo was still reeling from, he felt ashamed that he was fancying the man's appearance.

After twisting and turning through dark side streets and unsavory neighborhoods, Fabbiano pointed to a tall, thin red-, white-, and blue-striped post, mounted on an angle to a large wired pole. "*Barbiere*," Fabbiano said, and he disappeared inside.

Paolo found it strange that the man would choose now to get a shave and a haircut. He actually didn't know whether he was supposed to follow or wait on the street. Soon, a man in white pants, a white shirt, and a thin red tie motioned to him from the doorway. Paolo followed him inside.

"Put the bags down. Someone will tend to them," Fabbiano said with his back to Paolo. "I'll just be a minute." He vanished behind a felt curtain at the back of the shop.

Paolo smiled awkwardly at the man in white, who ignored him. Looking around, he noticed that all of the men were dressed identically—white pants, white shirts with sleeves rolled up to the elbow, thin red ties, and black belts. Several were attending to patrons. And the rest stood motionless by red leather chairs with padded leg, arm, and headrests. Near the back was a large open cupboard with row after row of porcelain shaving mugs, each hand-painted with the name of a regular patron.

There were eight chairs, four on each side of the shop. Paolo counted sixteen large mirrors with ornate mahogany frames. Except for a small amount of hair about the floor, the place was immaculate. Hair creams and oils and combs and scissors were lined up neatly at each station. Three gentlemen draped with white aprons were reclining in chairs. One had a towel over his face. Another was being shaved. The third, lying almost flat, was having his hair cut. At the same time, a young bootblack in high stockings lifted one of the man's legs and placed his foot on a portable shoe rest made of wood and iron. From there, the bootblack proceeded to apply cream to the man's boot.

Fabbiano emerged from the back, accompanied by a very short, stocky man who was dressed like the others except for the addition of a black waistcoat. He puffed on something gnarled and dark that looked more like a twig than a cigar.

"So," the man said, eyeing Paolo, "you are our little *Santa Ana* stowaway from Palermo. Let's have a look." He stood uncomfortably close. The smoke burned Paolo's eyes. "You say he is a clever boy, Fabbiano?"

"Yes, Nicolo, quite clever. And very appreciative of our help, right, Paolo?" Fabbiano's words seemed more like a statement than a question.

"Yes, signore, I am very thankful to be here," Paolo managed to say.

"You like the smell of hair tonic and boot cream, Signorino Paolo?" the man asked. "Get used to it. You'll be living upstairs."

"I have no money to pay, signore," Paolo said.

"You leave that up to Nicolo Bertolino," the man said with a smile. "We will talk later. Take your little paper valise. In the very back there are stairs. Go to the third floor. You will find Signora Alessi. She will show you to your room and tell you about washroom privileges. And she will teach you English and instruct you about the currency. Your lessons begin immediately. Go now. Later, we will talk."

Paolo hesitated and then grabbed his valise and headed to the back.

The two men looked after him.

"So … you bring me more than girls this trip, Fabbiano. Very good. Very good, indeed," Nicolo said with a laugh. He patted Fabbiano on the back. "Your car will be here momentarily." He turned to one of the barbers. "Pietro! Take Signore Fabbiano's bags to the street and wait with them until the car arrives."

The young man sprang to action.

"Fabbiano, we must have dinner this week. I will ring you up. We have much to discuss," Nicolo said.

"I will wait for your call. Now I must rid my skin of *Santa Ana*'s filth. Ciao, my friend," Fabbiano said, waving as he exited the shop.

Nicolo waved back. "Welcome back to America, Fabbiano."

"Franco, do not drag the bag. It will tear. Look, you are dragging it. Franco!" Giuseppe was about to abandon whatever scrap of patience remained after the last two weeks. He was sick. He was dirty. He was exhausted. And every time he looked at his son, Franco reminded him of the wife he had left behind in Serra San Bruno. Clearly, he was taking it all out on the boy.

"Here, let me show you a better way," Giuseppe said in a lighter voice as he adjusted the cloth bag across Franco's shoulder. "Now ... isn't that better?"

Franco nodded. The two made their way across the three-meter boardwalk that had been crudely placed between the ferry and the dock. Giuseppe fumbled for the paper he had wrapped around Marianna's picture. He unfolded it and slowly pointed at the letters. Then he remembered. "Rodolfo Moretti," he quietly said. "Rodolfo Moretti."

When he looked up, the multitude of people welcoming passengers was almost overwhelming. How was he to find this man?

"Papa, you must call the name," Franco said.

"What? What do you mean?" Giuseppe asked.

"Remember, Zia Annunziata told us—'When you are permitted in L'America, when you leave the water, you must shout the *padrone*'s name.' Shout. Shout it, Papa," Franco said encouragingly.

"*Va bene.* Okay," Giuseppe said. "What a good memory you have." One last time he whispered the name. He looked around. Many were already calling out names. He smiled at Franco. "Rodolfo Moretti!" he shouted. "Moretti! Rodolfo Moretti!"

Franco yelled as well. "Moretti! Rodolfo Moretti!"

They laughed. They screamed. At times they even sang the name. Franco loved the game. For the first time since they left Calabria, the two were amusing themselves.

"Mosca!" a voice in the distance called. "Mosca!" The voice grew louder.

"Papa, do you hear?" Franco asked.

"Yes, yes," Giuseppe answered, his eyes examining the dock. "Moretti!" he called.

"Sì, Mosca," a man's voice answered from only meters away. And then, from behind a large group of people exchanging enthusiastic greetings, a well-dressed gentleman appeared. He wore a checked suit, a solid waistcoat, and a white shirt with a high, rounded collar and colorful tie. He had a prominent mole on his right cheek and a slight twitch that, in Giuseppe's mind, had to be related to that large, dark protuberance.

Giuseppe feared the worst, but this was Zia Annunziata's doing, so he approached.

"Giuseppe Mosca?" the man said as he held out his hand.

"Sì," Giuseppe replied, shaking the man's hand. "Signore Moretti?" he asked.

"But of course," the man answered. "And this must be Franco," he continued, bowing. "You are just as your *zia* described." He laughed. "Welcome to America, Giuseppe and Franco Mosca!"

◆

Claudio, now alone with his stable, was feeling full of himself and his latest accomplishments. After all, not only had he returned this trip with a particularly fetching inventory, but he also had been instrumental in snaring a young Sicilian for his employer. It had been a good trip indeed.

Claudio raised a handful of papers skyward. "Ladies, you will soon enter L'America and begin to seek your fortune. But before that, one more piece of business." He knocked on the door behind the bench. It opened, and a Catholic priest appeared. The priest carried a notebook in his hand.

"Come see the padre," Claudio ordered. "Make your mark in his book. Come, come. It is painless."

As each woman approached, Claudio placed a pen in her hand, and the priest offered her a page in the book, where each woman signed her name or crudely scribbled an "x." When they were finished, Claudio handed the priest an envelope, and just as quickly, the man of the cloth was gone.

Claudio turned to the group of young men who had stood before the judge moments ago. "Gentlemen, you are free to go," he instructed. "You will be paid by the man in the white hat just outside the door. Go now. Go."

The twenty men made their way back through the double doors.

"There you have it," said Claudio. "L'America opens its doors to the newly married woman. Once she is through, the church annuls the marriage, and you are free to work for Signore Fabbiano as single women. Welcome to L'America!"

CHAPTER 14

By day... [Mulberry Street] was a purgatory of unrelieved squalor,
at night an inferno tenanted by the very dregs of humanity, where
the new arrivals lived in damp basements, leaky garrets, clammy
cellars and out houses and stables converted into dwellings.
—Jacob Riis, *How the Other Half Lives*

Between 1870 and 1915, the population on the Lower East Side of
Manhattan tripled. With 76 percent of the residents foreign-born,
the streets were not only teeming; they were volatile. Jews, Russians,
Austro-Hungarians, Dutch, English, Irish, Germans, and Italians all vied
for lodging, work, tolerance, and homeland familiarity. In the square
block formed by Harry Howard Square and Baxter, Bayard, and Mulberry
Streets, hundreds upon hundreds of souls took daily to the streets, choosing

crowded sidewalks and avenues over the claustrophobia of dark and musty tenements.

It was no wonder. Most rooms available to immigrants were undersized, with as many as eight or ten sleeping in close quarters. The beds were usually thin mattresses supported by rusty metal frames. A few nails were tacked on the walls, from which hung their shoddy clothes. If they were lucky, they shared a hot plate, where very modest meals were warmed. The pots they used doubled as wash basins. There was nothing for them here. Tempers often flared. Mistrust abounded. Scoundrels manhandled the timid.

"Papa, I don't think we left the boat," Franco moaned.

"Why? Do you still feel sick?" Giuseppe asked.

Franco looked around the room the *padrone* had arranged for them. He couldn't understand. So many in such a small space. Even the hut in Serra had seemed so much larger than this. And it was eerily quiet—and profoundly sad. Though almost no one uttered a sound, the faces seemed to shout at Franco. The men were weather-beaten, the women anxious and suspicious. And none of the children made eye contact. Their heads were bowed, as though they preferred the companionship of damp floorboards.

"I don't think I like L'America, Papa."

Giuseppe frowned.

"I'm sorry, Papa."

"What did I tell you when Signore Moretti was kind enough to find us a place to live?" Giuseppe asked.

"We must be grateful to God. Whatever dirt he asks us to work with, we must sift it through our hands ..." Franco hesitated.

"Lovingly, as if it were the richest soil on earth," Giuseppe said.

"Lovingly," Franco said as he looked about.

Giuseppe smiled to himself. He appreciated his son's sarcasm. But instruction was so important, especially given Franco's tenuous age. He had seen so many of the young turn from the church, from respect, and from the wisdom of their elders. The uncertainty of Italy's future had a lot to do with that. And until his son Stefano's own rebellion, Giuseppe had been quick to place the blame on parents. He could do no more for his eldest, but Franco was still in his shadow.

"Go to sleep, my son. We must meet Signore Moretti very early tomorrow. He promises work. Then ... then you will feel like a man, I promise you. *Buono note, uomo della mia.*"

"I am your man, Papa?" Franco asked eagerly.

"*E vero,*" Giuseppe replied. "It is true."

———◆———

The shifting from one mode of transportation to another was taking its toll on the Grimaldis. Upon disembarking the *Santa Ana* in New York, they had believed their miserable journey was over. But they had soon found themselves on another boat to Ellis Island and then another back to New York City. Still another ferry had transported them from New York City's Liberty Street Ferry Terminal to the Central Railroad complex along the waterfront in Jersey City.

The one-and-a-half-mile terminal had been built in the 1880s in Communipaw Cove, better known for its oyster beds and marsh grass, which were replaced by a sprawling, red-brick, three-story Victorian-style head terminal. With its steep pitched roof, third-floor dormers, arched windows, cupola, and clock tower, the massive structure was impressive indeed. Inside, the concourse was a maze of English buff-colored glazed brick walls. Outside, hydraulic bridges constructed of iron and wood directed commuters to those godforsaken ferries. The Central Railroad of

New Jersey logo, with the Statue of Liberty at its center, sparkled above the phrase "Gateway to the West."

Aldo stood gazing up at the ceiling of the waiting room. It was supported by huge, red iron trusses.

"Pretty impressive, this America, eh, nephew?" Roberto chuckled.

"You see how the trusses are built from angle iron?" Aldo observed. "They can support more weight than wood. This allows the roof to be so much wider, so open. Look there. They are riveted, bolted, *and* welded. And the design—it looks like an enormous starburst."

"You see, Aldo, that is why you are here. We will someday make beautiful buildings together in America!" Roberto said, slapping Aldo on the back.

"Where is the peanut roaster?" Salvatore asked.

"You will see it soon enough, Sal," Gianni answered.

"Sal?" Salvatore questioned.

"That is what they will call you here in America. We don't use long names anymore," Carlo added.

Salvatore looked up at Anna. "Mama, I am Sal now. I have an American name. What is yours?"

"I don't think I have one … Sal," Anna laughed.

"Oh, but you do. Of course, you do," Teresa said. "It is Anne. You see? Shorter."

"I don't like that," Aldo said.

"You will get used to it, nephew," Roberto insisted. "And look … Sal. We have found the peanut roaster." He pointed.

They had all arrived at track number 8. Car after car, as far as the eye could see, stood motionless next to the passenger boarding area. The shiny steel with words the Grimaldis could not read seemed to disappear into a fog further down the track.

"Thirteen," Salvatore said.

"What is thirteen?" Aldo asked.

"They all have thirteen windows," Salvatore announced. "Will we sit next to a window?"

"You will see many wonderful things, Sal," Gianni said. "Just you wait."

"It doesn't look like a peanut roaster," Salvatore said with a frown.

"Ahhh, the peanut roaster." Gianni smiled. "I will show it to you. We have time. May I take him to it, Aldo?"

Aldo turned to Roberto, who nodded.

Gianni and Salvatore quickly stepped into the haze. When they emerged on the other side, a giant iron monster was waiting. Belching white smoke, the matte black Baldwin steam engine was beautifully accented by its silver-rimmed wheels and piston valves. Dwarfed by the mammoth, Salvatore was awestruck.

"Look there," Gianni said, pointing to the top. A man in a blue and gray shirt and matching cap sat with his arm across an open window. "You see him? That is the hog jockey."

"This America has such funny names," Salvatore laughed.

Gianni bent down and looked at his cousin for a moment. "Cousin, I am jealous of you."

"Jealous, Gianni? Of me?" Salvatore was incredulous.

"You have no idea what awaits you. Everything is new. Everything.

So … let's go back to the others, climb aboard this peanut roaster, and start your adventure."

"Does the hog jockey know the way?" Salvatore asked.

"Yes. Yes, he does," Gianni said with a smile.

———◆———

Signora Alessi placed a quarter on the table. Paolo stared at her. She was a slight woman, with grey hair held in a tight bun. Her dark eyes flashed from the table to Paolo and back to the table again. She tapped her foot impatiently.

"Well, Mr. Paolo? What is it?" she demanded.

Paolo thought a moment more. Wrong answers had consequences—Signora Alessi's consequences. They were stupid and childish. And yet he was afraid of this little woman.

"*Venti centesimi*," he stuttered.

"No!" she shouted. "Give me your hand."

He slowly extended his right hand, palm up, and placed it on the table.

She produced a thin switch made from the branch of a maple tree. She lashed it twice across his hand. "In … English!"

"I am not five years old!" Paolo shouted. "You cannot make me learn with a damn stick."

"In English," she said. "And without the disrespectful language."

"This is ridiculous. In the short time I've been on the street, I've heard more Italian than English."

"And that's why they are on the street," she retorted. "In English. Twenty-five cents."

"Towenty ... fiva ... centes," he said, struggling with the pronunciations.

"And do you want more than twenty-five cents, Mr. Paolo?" she asked.

"*Como?*" he asked.

She stared at him blankly.

"What?" he asked, this time in English.

"*Cosa vuoi di piu?*" she repeated. "Do you want more?"

"Sì. Yessa. Yessa. I ... a ... wanta ... *piu.*"

"More!" she said.

"Mora," he said.

"Then you must learn English," she said. "Listen to me. Signore Bertolino is a wonderful man. He took me in when I was on the street—on the street. My husband and son were killed by a runaway horse carriage, left in the dirt road to die, right outside these walls. Nobody helped. Signore— he come out of his shop with towels and antiseptics. He tried. But there was too much blood, too much dirt. We had nothing, not two nickels. And no family. Signore Bertolino paid for the coffins and the priest. If Signore takes you in, you are blessed. You should be on your knees to the Madonna."

"*Mi dispiace,*" Paolo said, embarrassed.

"In English," she scolded.

"Ima ... saw ... ree," he said, still struggling.

"*Molto buono,*" Signora Alessi said.

"In English," Paolo teased.

"Very good," she said with a smile.

CHAPTER 15

Those masterful images, because complete
Grew in pure mind, but out of what began?
A mound of refuse, of the sweepings of a street,
Old kettles, old bottles, and a broken can,
Old iron, old bones, old rags, that raving slut
Who keeps the till. Now that my ladder's gone
I must lie down where all ladders start
In the foul rag-and-bone shop of the heart.
—William Butler Yeats, "The Circus Animals' Desertion"

Franco, come, you must wake up." Giuseppe shook his son, who was slow to respond.

"What? Papa, it is dark. Why?" Franco finally roused.

"Time for work, Signore Franco. Doesn't that sound good? Time for work?" Giuseppe asked.

"It would sound better three hours from now," Franco moaned.

"Oh, the working man makes a joke," Giuseppe chuckled.

"We work in the night?" Franco sat up, rubbing his eyes.

"Signore Moretti said that we must get to the cellar before dawn. That way, we will have the biggest and best collection," Giuseppe said, handing Franco his pants.

"What collection, Papa?"

"I do not know."

"And we will be working in a cellar?" Franco asked.

"Again, I do not know. He gave me an address. The sooner we go, the sooner we find out."

Giuseppe and Franco shivered in the cold. The late-October predawn gusts assaulted them in waves as they dodged the merchants who were already stacking their wooden crates of fruits and vegetables and positioning their carts on Bayard. High above them, as far as the eye could see, rope lines of clothes stretched from window to window. Most of the women washed and pressed their family's limited supply very early in the day. Soon, the streets would be teeming with disoriented tenants attempting to shake off the effects of another cramped and putrid night.

They turned the corner onto Baxter. Giuseppe searched his jacket pocket and retrieved a folded piece of paper, which he handed to Franco. "This is the number," he said.

"Two-six-two," Franco answered. "Look, the numbers are on the walls."

The two carefully inspected each and every address along Baxter until they found 262. It was a four-story brick building with a single door. There were five sets of dusty windows on each of the upper floors, but no one was about. It did not appear to Giuseppe that this was an apartment building, so he knocked at the door. There was no answer. He knocked again, this time with his fist. He shrugged his shoulders at Franco.

"*Cosa vuoi?*" a muffled male voice finally called from inside. "What do you want?"

Giuseppe pressed his lips close to the door. "Signore Moretti sent us."

"Who?" The man's voice sounded impatient.

"Moretti, *il padrone.* For work," Giuseppe replied.

"Why didn't you say so in the first place?" the man answered. "Look to your left, those wooden doors on the sidewalk. Just go down. Now let me sleep."

Franco pointed to what appeared to be an outside cellar entrance. Next to it, leaning against the brick wall, was a large wooden cart with four wheels. Giuseppe smiled, remembering his own cart back home. How he wished he were lugging it up the mountain with vegetables for Marianna.

"I think we found the cellar, Papa."

Giuseppe squatted down and struggled to lift one side. Suddenly, two arms appeared from below and threw open both doors. Giuseppe stumbled back.

An old woman in layered clothes and a scarf pulled tight around her head barked from behind the arms. "What do you want, signore?" she asked. "Who told you to open my doors?"

"I am Giuseppe Mosca," he said, as though this would explain everything.

The woman eyed him carefully and then spit on the sidewalk next to Giuseppe. "What is that to me? I don't know you." She turned and called out behind her. "Mosca! *Che conosce* Mosca? Who knows Mosca?"

From the darkness of the cellar, a man replied, "Rodolfo Moretti *lo mando!*"

"Sì, sì, sì. Signore Moretti sent me," Giuseppe said.

"And you have a helper. That's good," the woman said, nodding. "There is your cart. I'll get the boy a basket, and you can be on your way." She disappeared back into the cellar.

"Papa, are we going to pick vegetables? I think it is too cold for vegetables. Where will we find them?"

"Soon we will find out everything. But we have a cart. And it looks like a good one," Giuseppe said as he inspected the wheels.

The woman pushed a large wicker basket through the opening. It was crudely constructed and nearly a meter deep, with a wide opening. On one side were two leather straps. "Here, the boy can use a basket. Inside is a hook," she said.

Giuseppe and Franco looked at her blankly.

"You know nothing, do you?" She shook her head and emerged from the cellar, grabbing the basket from Giuseppe. "Turn around, boy."

Franco reluctantly turned his back to her, never taking his eyes from his father.

The woman pulled his arms through the straps. The contraption now hung awkwardly from his back. She reached into the basket and pulled out a long wooden stick with a metal hook on one end. She handed it to

Franco. "There you go. Congratulations. You're now a rag-and-bone man," she announced.

"Rag-and-bone?" Franco didn't like the sound of that.

"You and your father will work the streets. He will pull the cart. You will carry the basket. Pick up everything you see. You never know. We will decide. When the cart is full, come back here and knock. You will be paid when we sort through and see what we can sell," she said. She immediately started back down the cellar stairs.

"Wait, please," Giuseppe said. "I'm not sure I understand. What are we looking for?"

She smiled wryly. "You are Calabrese, no?"

He nodded.

"That's what I thought. I said you will pick up everything—paper, broken glass, scraps of cloth, metal, whatever you see. We pay you for what we can salvage. Put it in the basket. Dump it in the cart. You are rag-and-bone men."

"Why bone men?" Franco asked.

"You bring the dead animals too—dogs, cats, rats, whatever. We can skin them for the fur. And we sell the bones for knife handles. Now go. Already your competition is at work."

◆

Paolo's lessons were progressing nicely. In spite of his early skirmishes with Signora Alessi, the two had become quite close. *Madre ha perso*, she called herself. His lost mother. He listened for hours to her stories. Sometimes she would lament the passing of her homeland, for that was what she called it. When she spoke of emigration, the story was never that she had left Italy; it was always that Italy had left her. L'America had brought its share of pain and loss and loneliness—she desperately missed her husband—but she was convinced that there was no better place on earth. And she thanked the Blessed Mother every day for it. *Il regalo*, she called it—the gift.

More often than not, though, her stories were about New York, Lower Manhattan, the neighborhoods, the shops, and the restaurants—and the people, the wonderful people who had become her new family. "To them we owe our allegiance," she would say as she pointed. "Signore Bertolino, Signore Fabbiano—devote yourself to them. They are your family now."

Paolo found her tone curious when she referred to these men. There was affection for sure, as well as admiration. But it seemed laced with obedience.

More importantly, though, Paolo was learning English. He was a clever student, according to Signora Alessi. He had absorbed much in a very short time. And he challenged himself. Paolo knew that there was power in his ability to speak the language of L'America. He worked hard, day after day, week after week. From the couch of her sitting room, he would practice his pronunciation and definitions and currency, with the promise that one day he would be brought into Signore Bertolino's circle.

Signora Alessi rewarded him with more and more freedom. At night, he was allowed to walk the streets, visit the shops, and test his training. What she didn't know was how often he strayed outside the confines of the area surrounding Cuyler's Alley and headed north to a walk-up on Beekman Street, for that was the address Luisa Morosco had slid into his pocket before they parted on the *Santa Ana*.

Luisa was very good at giving her parents the slip when Paolo's whistle from the corner lamppost signaled his presence. More often than not, they would make their way two blocks north on Nassau, past the World Building, to the foot of the Brooklyn Bridge. They would hold hands, practice their English, and make up stories about the folks who traveled back and forth across the bridge. For more privacy, they'd cross Park Row and wander onto the grass of City Hall Park. In the dark, Paolo could be more intimate.

Occasionally, he would use the skills he had perfected in Palermo to steal her a bar of candy or someone's glass of Coca-Cola at a soda fountain. She delighted in his petty thievery. With a wry smile and an impish fondness for rebellion, she studied his every move. Eventually, she had begun to practice her own brand of cunning. Luisa's weapon of choice was distraction. With a heavy dose of makeup, she proved to be a very alluring partner. Her flirtations served them well.

Paolo had fallen hard for the fetching Luisa, and he loved the trysts and frivolous larceny, but he longed for the employ of Signore Bertolino. Signora Alessi counseled patience. But every day, he implored her to intervene. And every day, she wagged her finger at him.

"Signore knows about your progress. So he will know when the time is right. Trust him. Trust me," she would insist.

Eventually, Paolo stopped asking. Then one day, as if this was just what Bertolino had been waiting for, in the middle of Paolo's English recitation of Lincoln's Gettysburg Address, there was a knock at the door to Alessi's sitting room. She never had visitors, so Paolo looked at her curiously.

She smiled. "I believe that knock is for you, Paolo," she said.

He didn't understand.

"Open it, boy. Don't sit there like day-old fish."

Paolo opened the door to find Signore Bertolino. He did his best to suppress a smile. At first he didn't notice that the signore was carrying clothes on his arm—pants, shirt, jacket, and waistcoat. In his hand he carried a pair of high leather oxford boots.

Finally, Paolo managed to speak. "Signore Bertolino. Hello, sir."

"Signorino Paolo. Signora Alessi tells me your lessons are going very well. You should be proud. She is a tough taskmaster."

"I have learned so much from her. Thank you. Thank you for everything," Paolo said.

"Well, boy, stop staring. This suit is not going to put itself on," Bertolino said, holding out his arm.

"These are for me?" Paolo was astonished.

"Of course. My employees are gentlemen," Bertolino said.

"Your employees?" Paolo questioned.

"Oh, don't be *stupido*," Alessi blurted. "Now you make me look bad."

Paolo took the clothes. They were elegant. The brown suit was speckled with beige threads and delicate pinstripes. It had a matching waistcoat and a long frock coat. The shirt was heavily starched, there was a silk brown and beige tie, and the boots smelled of fine leather.

"So Signorino Paolo, I have your first assignment," Bertolino said. "Signora?" He motioned to the clothes.

Signora Alessi took the clothes from Paolo and moved a few steps away from the two men. It was clearly a sign of respect. Paolo looked after her.

"Look at me, young man. For now you leave the nipple, eh?" He laughed. "Here is a letter you must deliver to someone who has become a nuisance—Signore Ippolito. You know the milliner on the corner of Pearl and Fulton?"

Paolo looked at him uncertainly.

"Oh, come now, Paolo. You have passed it many times on your excursions to Beekman Street."

Paolo was caught off guard.

"Never mind that now," Bertolino said with a wave of his hand. "Come read the letter, and then you will sign it. Read it. I'll explain."

Paolo opened the envelope and unfolded a handwritten note.

"Aloud, Paolo. Aloud," Bertolino ordered.

Paolo read, "Signore Ippolito, we have been more than patient with you. But now it is time to stop ignoring our invoices. Please pay as you have been instructed, and you may continue to operate your shop without consequence. However, if our courier returns empty-handed, this very evening your beautiful hats will be consumed by an untimely fire."

"Very good," Bertolino said. "I like that … untimely fire. And now we sign in the large space at the bottom." He approached Paolo. "Hold out your hand."

Paolo obliged, and to his astonishment, Bertolino smeared his right hand with boot black.

"Now," the signore said, "make our mark on the paper." Signore Bertolino pressed Paolo's hand against the page and smiled. "*La Mano Nera*," he announced. "What do they say in Sicily, Signora Alessi?"

"*A Manu Niura*, signore," she answered. "The Black Hand."

Now Paolo allowed himself that smile. After all, this was why he had come. Pietro be damned. Paolo was about to make his mark in L'America.

"Signora Alessi, clean the boy up and show him how to tie the perfect knot," Bertolino instructed. "I'll be waiting downstairs."

———————◆———————

For hours, Salvatore sat with his nose pressed against the window. Even after the gas lamps above their red leather bench seats were lit, and the scenery became almost impossible to make out, he fought the darkness for any image. Aldo and Roberto spoke of construction opportunities the entire trip. Carlo slept. Anna and Teresa discussed American fashion. And Gianni watched after Salvatore.

Roberto produced a catalogue from his satchel. "Look. Look here, Aldo. The Sears and Roebuck Company's *Book of Modern Homes*. In America, this is how they buy their homes. From a magazine. See? Home number 52. That is what they call it. They ship everything to you. Look—millwork, siding, flooring, lumber, building paper, gutter, sash weights, mantel, hardware, lath, and shingles. From a department store, nephew!" Roberto was animated.

"Are you saying that is a good thing, Roberto?" Aldo questioned. "This is the L'American dream for me and my family? A house in a box?"

"Of course not. This is crap." Roberto pounded the page with his fist. "These are not builders. They're ... they're boors. Do you know what they have now in this country? Instant coffee. It's a powder you put in a cup of hot water. That is their coffee. And now ... instant houses."

"Why are you telling me this, Roberto?" Aldo was confused and concerned. "This is our big opportunity? This Mr. Sears?"

"Yes. Yes, it is," Roberto insisted. "But not how you think. You see these hands? They are a gift from God. You know my work."

"Yes, yes, *la Michaelangelo*. But no one can afford the Sistine Chapel anymore," Aldo said.

"You are right. Not in Italy. I have the hands. You have the brains. Together we will bring art to America. And that," Roberto announced, "is why you are here."

"Anne, we must go shopping," Teresa said. "Our skirts are now above the ankle. Can you believe it?"

"Are you serious, Teresa?" Anna was both intrigued and mildly aroused.

"Yes," Anna replied. "And if you dare, hobble skirts are all the rage."

"Hobble?" Anna struggled with the word.

"Wide at the hips and narrow at the ankle," Teresa explained. "You have to take very short steps, but they are so lovely. And listen, Anne"—Teresa lowered her voice to a whisper as she drew Anna close—"I have been wanting for months to bob my hair. Roberto will have none of it. But there is strength in numbers."

"Bob?" Anna questioned. "This country has such a strange language."

"The movie stars are now cutting their hair to their chin—and wearing straight bangs, right across the top of their eyebrows," Teresa said, giggling.

At every stop, Salvatore asked the same question: "Is this Kellisland?"

And at every stop, Gianni answered and corrected him: "No, and it is called Cleveland ... Cleve-land."

Albany, Schenectady, Utica, still not Cleveland. Syracuse, Richmond, Buffalo, Dunkirk, not Cleveland. But finally, after Westfield, Erie, and Ashtabula, it was Cleveland. As the tracks entered the city limits from the south, near Bradley Road, the mighty train wound its way through the Flats, a half-mile-wide valley along the Cuyahoga River. They passed iron furnaces, rolling mills, foundries, lumberyards, flour mills, and Whiskey Island, so named for its distillery and thirteen Irish saloons. From there, the train slowed as it squealed into the terminal.

When the train finally came to rest at the platform, it was as though someone had signaled for mass chaos. Docile passengers became manic. Bags and bundles were flung about without the least bit of concern for old or young.

Anna adjusted her hat and smoothed her coat. "Where are the attendants?" she asked. "Are we expected to carry our own bags?"

"Anna, my sweet," Aldo said, touching her arm, "we have been on this journey for nearly three weeks. Have you seen one attendant willing to personally transport a single piece of your luggage?"

"Well, I had hoped that the further away we got from that horrible boat, the more likely we were to find civilization," she answered.

Carlo leaned in. "Oh, we are quite civilized here, I can assure you, Anne. Just wait till you see the car that will carry you to the house. My friend Marco is bringing his new Ford Model T Coupelet. You and Mama will ride in style."

"See there, Anna? A motorcar," Aldo said encouragingly. "Thank you, Carlo. That will be wonderful."

◆

A very handsomely attired Paolo made his way down two flights of stairs to the barber shop. When he entered the room, it erupted in applause.

"See, Paolo, they approve," Bertolino said. "Very good. Very good indeed. But you are not complete." Signore Bertolino reached into a round box and retrieved a brown Stetson bowler derby hat. "Here, put this on."

Paolo obliged.

Bertolino adjusted the hat and stepped back to admire his handiwork. "Now ... now you are one of Bertolino's men," the signore announced. "And do you know what is funny? This hat was made by Ippolito. Can you imagine? So go—deliver your letter and begin your career. I have a feeling you are going to do very well."

Paolo turned and left the shop. Leaving Cuyler's Alley, on his first mission for *La Mano Nera*, his step was spirited. His heart was full.

CHAPTER 16

---

*Sono un vagabondo e semino parole
da un buco della tasca.*
I am a wanderer and sow words
from a hole in the pocket.
—Emanuel Carnevali

August 1916

The Calabrian sun hung high above the mountain. It was that merciless time of day. No matter how many times the dirt road twisted and turned during his ascent, Giuseppe could not avoid the searing heat. And today of all days, the cart was overflowing. Still, he didn't mind the struggle, for the harvest was very kind indeed.

"Wait till your mama sees the citrons," he called back to his son, who was trying to steady the load.

"The citrons?" Franco asked.

"*Certo*, sure, the citrons. Didn't you see how many? Just like the old days. I think this year will be our best. The factory in Livorno will pay us nicely for these, my son."

"No, Papa. There are no citrons," Franco moaned.

"Don't be silly, Franco. You can't even push the cart, it is so heavy."

"Papa!" Franco shouted.

Giuseppe stopped. The cart rocked slightly and came to rest. "What do you think we have been carrying up this damned hill all morning? Don't play with me, Franco. Look for yourself." He pulled back the canvas covering the bounty. He squinted at what lay piled there—rags and broken glass and twisted metal and dead cats.

"No citrons, Papa," Franco said.

Giuseppe sat up with a start. His clothes were drenched in sweat. His eyes burned with the moisture that had made its way down his forehead.

Franco was bent over him. "There are no citrons, Papa."

Giuseppe shook his head and touched Franco's cheek. "I'm sorry. I frightened you, my son. It was a stupid dream." He rubbed his eyes and thought a moment. "But maybe not so stupid. Get ready. We are going to see Signore Moretti."

"*Il padrone*, Papa?"

"Yes. You know that big factory we always pass on Mott Street? Where they make all the yarns and knitting things?" Giuseppe asked.

"Every time we walk by, you say Mama would love to go in there," Franco said.

"Moretti has been telling me for months that he will bring me to Signore Ulmann, the owner," Giuseppe said as he slid into his jacket.

"But you don't knit, Papa," Franco said.

"No. No, I don't. But this man loves beautiful suits. And I can make him beautiful suits, no?"

"Oh, Papa, of course you can. Everybody in Serra San Bruno knows that," Franco announced proudly.

"So maybe they need to know this in L'America," Giuseppe laughed.

Franco noticed a decidedly different gait as his father bounded up Baxter toward Harry Howard Square, where Rodolfo Moretti lived. Not since Serra San Bruno had Giuseppe seemed so animated and playful. And he was humming. At home in the mountains, he would sing at the top of his lungs, and his elegant tenor voice would echo for miles. Humming was a start, Franco thought. He was certain that his father would soon be crooning some old familiar folk songs, once he got a thimble on his finger.

When they arrived at the red brick walk-up, the front door was angled open. Giuseppe found that curious. Even in this neighborhood, where most were familiar and doors were left unlocked, it was unusual for one to be opened, even in the searing heat of summer. He instructed Franco to wait on the sidewalk and cautiously made his way inside.

In the hall, the reason for the open door became abundantly clear to Giuseppe. A group of women in long black skirts and veils sat sobbing in a row along the wall. The archway to Moretti's dining room was draped in black. No wonder Signore Moretti had been out of touch. Giuseppe worried that it might be his wife or, worse yet, one of his young children. He steadied himself and made his way into the dining room. A casket lay on top of the large table, which was covered in black crepe.

He was relieved that the box was obviously designed for an adult. He had been to too many funerals of the innocent—babies and children felled by diphtheria, typhoid, and scarlet fever, among other illnesses. He negotiated the crowded room and approached the casket. His heart burned when he was finally able to view the occupant. It was Rodolfo Moretti. But how? But why? Sure, Giuseppe felt horrible for the widow and her four children, but what was to happen to him now? Moretti had been his lifeline. Who would pay the landlord and keep him in work?

Giuseppe's eyes were fixed on the corpse. His breathing became labored when he thought about Signore Ulmann. A hand on his shoulder startled him, and he turned too quickly and awkwardly. Signora Moretti stumbled back. If not for the quick arms of a gentleman behind her, she would have fallen.

Teresina Moretti was a very slight woman who carried herself with dignity and grace. She was fond of spending the money her husband made, and her clothes were expensive and her makeup and hair meticulous.

"Signora, signora," Giuseppe cried out. "I am so sorry."

"Thank you, Giuseppe," she said as she regained her balance. "Thank you for coming."

"I did not know. I ... I was coming to see Signore. I did not know," he moaned.

"Oh, Giuseppe, it happened three days ago, two blocks from here. *Mio marito e stato girato.* He was shot. My husband was murdered. Why, Giuseppe, why?" she wailed. "Do you know something?"

"Of course not, Signora," he answered. "He was a good man. He was our only bridge between Serra and L'America. He was our bridge." Giuseppe could not hide his distress. "I was coming for an introduction to Signore Ulmann, so that I could make suits. I was going to make suits. I'm so sorry. I am rude. How could I even think of myself when you and your babies ..." His voice trailed off.

Teresina Moretti said nothing. She studied his face, brushed away her tears, and disappeared into the crowd of mourners without a word.

Giuseppe felt as though the entire room was judging him. He could not make his way back out onto the street fast enough. He found Franco sitting on the stoop, playing with his Tinkertoy. In one quick motion, he grabbed his son by the jacket, pulled him to his feet, and started down the street. "Put the toy away. It is time to grow up, Franco," Giuseppe chided.

Franco stuffed the toy into his jacket. "Why are we going this way?" Franco asked. "The needlework man's factory is the other way, Papa."

"Never you mind," Giuseppe snapped.

"Where are we going? What did Signore Moretti say?"

"You ask too many questions."

Giuseppe was struggling with an onslaught of emotions—fear, anger, despair. And to make matters worse, at times like this, he was desperate for the bosom of his Marianna. Oh, how he missed her love. She would know what to do, how to move forward. With each step, his legs grew heavier and heavier. He knew the pattern. Soon he would be frozen.

"This was a mistake, Franco. L'America was a mistake. Mama needs us, and I can send her almost nothing. I don't know what to plant, my son. I'm so sorry. I don't know what to plant …" Giuseppe's voice trailed off.

"I don't understand, Papa."

"Giuseppe," a voice called from behind them. "Signore Mosca."

They turned to see Teresina Moretti hurrying toward them. "Signore Mosca, why did you leave?" she asked.

"My son was outside. I didn't … I was …" he stammered.

"Here." She handed him a piece of paper.

He stared at it in his hand as if it were some foreign object, alien to him.

"It is for Signore Ulmann," she said. "Give it to his secretary when you arrive there. He will speak to you."

"Signora …" Giuseppe was incredulous.

"Say nothing, Signore Mosca. I knew a side of Rodolfo no one ever saw. In spite of his reputation, he actually cared for the ones who came to L'America. He spoke of you often, Giuseppe. He was certain you were a wonderful tailor."

"But he never saw my work, Signora."

"He saw your hands—the way you moved them, the way you buttoned a jacket. He often told me that one day you would be making suits. He said that he looked forward to the day he would be unable to afford them," she said.

"I don't understand." Giuseppe shook his head.

"You will. Go see Signore now, right now. And God be with you and your son." She touched Franco's shoulder, smiled at Giuseppe through swollen eyes, and walked away.

Giuseppe looked after her and then back at the paper.

"Signore Ulmann, Papa?" Franco asked.

"*E vero, il mio figlio*. It's true," he said. "But I cannot read the paper," he said sadly.

"No, of course you can't. But we know his factory. And he can read it, Papa. Signore Ulmann will read the paper."

"But look here," Giuseppe said, pointing to the paper. "What is that?"

Franco studied the word. "Bucilla. It says Bucilla," he said.

"But what is that? Bucilla?"

"Papa, what does it matter? Let's go!"

Ulmann and Company, also referred to as Bucilla, was an impressive brick structure on Mott Street. Founded in 1867 by European immigrant Bernard Ulmann, the company had grown from very humble beginnings to emerge as a leader in the industry. It made yarns for embroidering, sewing, knitting, lacemaking, braiding, and crocheting. In addition, it was widely known for publishing instructional books on needlework and knitting and even pattern books.

Giuseppe stood very still in front of the great building—or least to him it was great. And there was that word again: Bucilla. On the sign above the door. He didn't understand. For him, this L'America was overwhelming and confusing and frightening, and simple things, such as this word Bucilla, made him feel like his feet were in concrete. Once again, he was at the edge of his garden, unable to decide what to plant.

"Go, Papa. Go in," Franco said, but his voice was drowned out by the words on the sign. "Papa!"

"Yes, yes, of course. But where is the door to Signore Ulmann?" Giuseppe said.

"Just go in. Show the paper. They will tell us," Franco insisted.

"You take it, Franco. You show them."

Franco felt awkward but determined as he physically moved his father through the door and into the lobby.

The lobby was lined with lighted cabinets displaying the materials Ulmann manufactured. There were also framed pictures everywhere— pictures of machinery, factory workers, pallets of boxes. But Giuseppe's eyes were drawn to just one photo. On the curb of a crowded city street stood a young man smiling broadly beside a cart piled with fabric.

"May I help you?" a woman asked from behind a glass enclosure. She was rather young, but her glasses and the way she wore her hair piled high on her head could give unsuspecting souls the impression of middle-aged maturity. Giuseppe was caught off guard by this woman girl.

"We have a paper," Franco finally said, lifting his hand to the glass. "A paper for Signore Ulmann."

She took the note, read it, and looked back at Giuseppe, whose head was bowed. He was more at ease studying the patterns in the linoleum floor.

"I will be right back," the young woman said. "But I must warn you— Mr. Ulmann is a very busy man."

"Then we will come back," Giuseppe said quickly. He actually felt relieved.

"No. Wait here," she said and disappeared.

"Maybe we should not be here, Franco," Giuseppe moaned.

"Papa." Franco's voice was uncommonly stern. "We must stay."

Giuseppe was still unsure.

"You must stay for Mama," Franco said.

Giuseppe felt ashamed. He instinctively drew his son close to him and held on tight. Franco squirmed. Giuseppe thought about the last letter he had received from home. His baby angel, Adelina, had fallen ill. But Marianna, as usual, had assured him that she had everything under control. She said that their daughter's fevers had begun to subside, and she was certain the redness about her neck and face were due to how hot the sun had been this summer on the mountain. Still, Giuseppe prayed to San Bruno for protection.

"Mr. Ulmann will see you now," the young woman suddenly said. Giuseppe hadn't even noticed she had returned.

They were ushered down a long, paneled hallway lined by wooden doors with frosted glass windows. Each door was painted with a gold three-digit number. Franco was wide-eyed, Giuseppe uncertain. At the end of the hall, the receptionist opened a larger door, motioned them inside, and left, closing the door behind her.

A man Giuseppe assumed to be Bernard Ulmann rose from behind a large mahogany desk. "Mr. Mosca," he said, holding out his hand. "Welcome."

Giuseppe shook the man's hand. He was surprised at how small it was. As a matter of fact, it wasn't until Ulmann came around the corner of the desk that Giuseppe realized how short he was too. Ulmann was a stout, balding man with a thin white mustache and rimless glasses. He was dressed in a brown linen suit and a white shirt with a starched, rounded collar. His black silk tie was held together just below the knot with a rhinestone pin.

"So … very bad business, this shooting," Ulmann said. "I've known Teresina and Rodolfo a long time. We must pray for the children."

"Yes, San Bruno look after them," Giuseppe said.

"San Bruno?" Ulmann asked.

"Sì. His name is on our village in Calabria. We go to San Bruno for all our petitions," Giuseppe explained.

"Then go to him, you must," Ulmann said. "And who might this be?" he asked, patting Franco on the shoulder.

"My name is Franco Pietro Mosca," Franco blurted before Giuseppe could answer.

Ulmann chuckled. "Where do you work, Mr. Mosca?"

Giuseppe did not know how to answer.

"Everywhere, Signore Ulmann," Franco finally answered. "We are rag-and-bone men."

"Rag-and-bone men?" Ulmann asked Giuseppe incredulously.

All Giuseppe could manage was an apologetic nod.

"But you are a tailor," Ulmann stated.

"Yes, but … a long time ago … in Serra. In Italia," Giuseppe said.

"Tell me about my suit," Ulmann said, motioning to his attire.

"Signore?" Giuseppe asked.

"My suit. Tell me what is wrong."

"Signore, I cannot," Giuseppe said.

"You want to make me a suit? Tell me about this one," Ulmann insisted.

Giuseppe thought a moment. He did not want to offend. He did not want to appear arrogant. But he did not want to disappoint Marianna—and Franco and Adelina and Stefano.

"Well, signore," he finally said, "a suit must flatter your strengths and hide your … weaknesses." He looked to Ulmann for a response.

"Go on," Ulmann said.

"Okay, well … you are a …"

"Short, fat man," Ulmann said.

"This is a four-button suit, signore," Giuseppe said, trying to ignore Ulmann's statement. "Three buttons give more height. And the notches on the lapel do the same thing. They should be higher on a man of your ... build. And I would have given you no cuffs on the pants with a half break for the same reason. May I see the vent in the back of your suit coat?" he asked.

Ulmann turned around.

"You see, *mi dispiace* ... I'm sorry, but you must have vents, signore. They will prevent wrinkling on such a jacket. And there should be two of them, so that ..." He trailed off.

"So that my big backside can breathe?" Ulmann laughed.

"They give you room, signore," Giuseppe said.

"So you think you can make me tall and thin, Signore Mosca?" Ulmann asked.

Franco laughed.

"Franco!" Giuseppe admonished.

"No, it is fine, Mr. Mosca. He is right. And so are you. So ... make me this suit again."

"Signore?" Giuseppe didn't understand.

"Clearly, this suit is all wrong. I love the material. I love the color. But we cannot have me looking short and fat. I must be tall and thin. Right, Mr. Franco?" Ulmann said, grinning at the boy. He pulled open a drawer in a sideboard against the wall. The drawer was filled with fabric samples. He sorted through them and found his tan linen. "Here you go," he said, handing the sample to Giuseppe. "This is the one. Come back here tomorrow morning with a tape. You have a tape measure, Mr. Mosca?"

"Yes ... yes, I do. It is with my things. But tomorrow we are expected to fill our cart again."

"I know a little something about carts, Mr. Mosca," Ulmann said. "Thirty-five years ago, I pulled one from Stuyvesant to Soho and back again, seven days a week. Handkerchiefs and doilies, three for a penny—that's how I started. Rag-and-bone men—that's how you started. Tonight you take the cart back. Tomorrow you make my suit. After I put it on, we will talk."

"Signore, I don't understand," Giuseppe said.

"Don't worry. Tomorrow you will," Ulmann said. "Now go see Rebecca out front. She will give you money for the cloth and thread. You can use one of my machines."

"Oh, signore, *mi dispiace*, but I cannot use your machine," Giuseppe said apologetically.

"Nonsense. They sit idle."

"No, signore, I sew from hand. No machine," Giuseppe insisted.

"Well then, no machine, Mr. Mosca. See you in the morning." Ulmann escorted them to the door.

Neither Giuseppe nor Franco spoke as they walked the long hallway back to the lobby. Giuseppe was afraid that words might somehow change this new course. And Franco simply followed his father's lead—until he thought about the cart.

"So, Papa, we are no longer rag-and-bone men?" he finally asked.

"We will see, my son," Giuseppe answered. "We will see." He suppressed a smile as they approached Rebecca's window.

CHAPTER 17

The people yes.
The people will live on.
The learning and blundering people will live on.
They will be tricked and sold and again sold
And go back to the nourishing earth for rootholds,
The people so peculiar in renewal and comeback,
You can't laugh off their capacity to take it.
The mammoth rests between his cyclonic dramas.
—Carl Sandburg, "The People Yes"

By 1916, nearly twenty thousand people had emigrated from Mezzogiorno to the shores of Lake Erie. Six neighborhoods had already formed in Cleveland, with more on the way. Big Italy, the largest, was located along Woodland and Orange Avenues, from East Ninth to East Fortieth St. Little Italy, at Mayfield and Murray Hill roads, boasted an Italian-born population of 96 percent. Collinwood had a substantial settlement on the east side. And there were two on the west side, one near Clark and Fulton Avenue and one on Detroit, near West Sixty-Fifth. The last, and smallest, grew up around St. Marian Church.

These communities tended to congregate along lines largely defined by occupation. Big Italy became the center of the city's fruit industry since many of the settlers came from Sicily. It was here that Frank Catalano introduced Cleveland to oranges, olive oil, figs, anchovies, and garlic. In Little Italy, stonecutters flourished. Seizing the opportunity for monument work in Lake View Cemetery, Joseph Carabelli established what eventually became the city's leading marble and granite works. Tailors worked in the garment industry. Landscapers tended to estates. And almost all who could read scoured the pages of *La Voce Del Popolo Italiano*. *La Voce* interpreted American law, emphasized citizenship, and offered news from the homeland. It was the first newspaper in the country to publish articles in both English and Italian.

After ten months of sharing the family's four-room flat on Race Street, in the three-story tenement known as the Ginney Block, Roberto Micheli was finally able to secure an apartment for Aldo and Anna in the same complex in Little Italy. Built by the Newcomb brothers, this three-story, red brick building covered a half city block. For ten dollars a month, the Grimaldis settled into two small windowless bedrooms, a kitchen, a front room, and a closet with a commode on a raised platform and flush box overhead. There was a cold water tap in the kitchen and a coal- and wood-burning stove, for both heat and cooking. Light was provided by a single gas jet in each room. And to Aldo and Anna, this was heaven.

The families had grown close in those months of living together. Gianni and Carlo had taken charge of the Americanization of "Sal." They helped him with English and baseball. Soon he was disappearing for hours, joining the other boys in an abandoned coal yard at the far west end of the block, where they fashioned a baseball diamond out of stones and wood.

"Ann" and Theresa (who insisted on being called Terry) became inseparable. Though fifteen years Anna's elder, Theresa seemed so much younger to Anna. She was vibrant and clever, and her enthusiasm was contagious. The day the Grimaldis moved out, the two sobbed for hours.

"It's one damn flight of stairs," Aldo barked. "We're not going back to Naples. Don't be ridiculous."

That made them cry all the more. Aldo threw his arms in the air much like he often did whenever they would giggle and whisper in the corner. "You're schoolgirls," he would chide. "I bring you to L'America to go forward, not backward."

"America!" they would yell back at him in unison. "A-merica."

If there was any conflict between the families, it was the Michelis' insistence on complete assimilation and Aldo's rebellion.

"You must accept that you are in America now, nephew," Roberto would scold. "If you are to make your name in this new country, you must shake off some of the old country. It's a fact."

"I will not make my name by changing it … Robert," Aldo would spit, as though his uncle's Americanized name was some sort of slur.

"Suit yourself. I am building the colonnade at the new city hall, and you cut stones for the cemetery. *Questo e bene*? This is okay with you?"

"Signore Carabelli will be making me a foreman soon," Aldo said.

"Joseph Carabelli Jr. is only a boy. He is not his father, God rest his soul," Roberto said, crossing himself.

"Still, he has faith in me. And in case you haven't noticed, he runs the company," Aldo retorted.

"So you will boss other boys who will make gravestones. That is not all you can be in this world, nephew. Washington, DC, this nation's capital—look at what is happening there. Italians built the Union Station. You have seen pictures of Bernasconi's statues on the facade. Vincent Palumbo from Molfetta and Roger Morigi, Milanese—they were the artists who worked on Washington's National Cathedral. And do you see what the Piccirilli brothers are doing in Washington? A President Lincoln Memorial."

"But you bring me to this Cleveland."

"You are missing the point."

———————◆———————

Although the means were small and the comforts few and far between, the Michelis and Grimaldis were often reminded of just how blessed they were, given the plight of the typical immigrant. In and around the Hiram House in Big Italy, for example, things were very different. The settlement was an attempt at assisting immigrants with social services, language classes, vocational training, and the like. In truth, it was a hotbed of ethnic clashes, particularly among Italians and Jews. It was home to a Jewish-Slovak gang called the Zookeys and a band of hooligans known as Joe Amato and the Robber Gang. And the many saloons surrounding the project were frequented by infamous characters such as Frog Island Kate, Babe Downs, and Old Mother Witch.

In the weeks that followed their move upstairs at Ginney Block, things appeared to finally shift in the Grimaldis' favor. Joseph Carabelli did, in fact, promote Aldo to foreman, which meant better pay, better hours, and less dust. He was able to provide Anna with some modest conveniences and one or two items with which to pamper herself. Aldo even convinced himself that some American clothing for Salvatore would help his adaptation in this L'America.

Uncle Roberto was relentless, though. He was bound and determined to drag Aldo, albeit kicking and screaming, into American culture. Of course, there was an ulterior motive. Aldo's talent could be realized only if it was accompanied by better English and a better understanding of his adopted country.

◆

On one particularly hot night, Carlo's friend Marco brought his Ford Model T Coupelet around. Salvatore was mesmerized by the shiny black machine, with its single door, gold grille, and white tires with black spokes. Aldo, Anna, Theresa, and Roberto were a few paces away, standing at the bottom of one of the Block's five stairways, trying to catch any hint of a breeze.

"Don't just look at it, little man," Marco said. "Climb inside."

Salvatore needed no urging as he bounced his way into the driver's seat.

"No, not there," Carlo laughed. "In the back. Only Marco drives this beautiful lady."

"We are going for a ride?" Salvatore asked.

"Absolutely," Marco answered. "Robert, Terry, bring Al and Ann. We must go to the park."

"The park?" Aldo asked.

"It's the only place to get some relief from this blessed heat," Roberto explained as he ushered the Grimaldis into the car, not waiting for any objections.

In a matter of minutes, the vehicle was motoring its way down Race Street, its passengers crammed inside like livestock.

"Is it safe to have so many?" Theresa asked.

"You'll thank Marco when we get to the park," Carlo said.

Situated on 122 acres on the city's east side, Gordon Park was adjacent to Lake Erie. A hillside ran down to the beach, but if you situated yourself near the crest of the bluff, you could catch the lake breeze in soothing waves. On nights such as this, it seemed most of Cleveland was there. Tonight, the travelers found the perfect spot. There was even a young man selling Cracker Jack nearby.

"Please, please, Papa. Can we get some Cracker Jack?" Salvatore pleaded.

"We are here for the breeze. We have plenty of things to eat at home," Aldo said.

"But it's Cracker Jack," Salvatore argued. "They have baseball cards inside."

"Stop it, Salvatore. I said you can eat at home if you're hungry."

"Signore Grimaldi, it is my fault," Marco said. "I told him about the Cracker Jack man on the way here. Please, if you don't mind, let me buy him a box."

Aldo stared at Marco, expressionless.

"I insist," Marco said finally.

"Salvatore will pay you back by doing something for you. He will help you clean your automobile."

"Perfect! I hate a dirty car," Marco shouted as he and Salvatore trotted off toward the Cracker Jack man.

"Thank you, *amore mio*," Anna whispered in Aldo's ear.

"I don't like when he begs. Grimaldis do not beg. They work for what they have," Aldo insisted.

"Have you thought about the classes, Al?" Roberto asked.

"Aldo," he said flatly.

"Well, have you?"

"Why is this necessary?" Aldo asked.

"It is not necessary. It is important."

"For what, Uncle? For what?"

"For your future—our future. Citizenship will open the doors. You must trust me on this. And you must join the Sons of Italy."

"I am not comfortable with clubs," Aldo said.

"This is more than a club. This is where you will meet the people you need to know to become successful here. It's a mutual aid society."

"Did you not hear what I told my son? We work. We do not take handouts," Aldo insisted.

"You are so stubborn you cannot see a meter in front of you. I am not talking about gifts. Let me ask you something, nephew. How well did you do on your own in Naples? How did that work?"

"They were the Camorra!" Aldo shouted.

"But this is a brotherhood of people who care for you, not of criminals. Do you have life insurance, nephew? Will someone pay Anna and Salvatore if something happens to you? I have four hundred dollars, just for being a member. And they will pay my funeral expenses."

"Does Theresa know this? I would be careful, Uncle."

"Papa! Papa!" Salvatore called as he ran toward them. "Papa, look!"

"What is it, Salvatore? Are you all right?" Aldo asked.

"Look. Look what I got inside the box!" Salvatore was out of breath.

Aldo looked at the square card he was handed. "What is this? Who is this?"

"Tris Speaker, Papa. Can you believe it? I got Tris Speaker!"

Aldo looked to Marco for some help.

"Tris Speaker is the center fielder for the Indians," Marco offered.

"The Grey Eagle, Papa," Salvatore laughed. "Everybody knows him."

"This was in the box of Cracker Jack?" Aldo asked Marco.

"They have baseball cards as prizes," Marco answered.

"They put these in with the food?" Aldo was incredulous.

"He's better than Ty Cobb. This is the best prize ever!" Salvatore exclaimed.

"This L'America is so hard to understand," Aldo said, shaking his head.

Roberto smiled. "That is why you have me, nephew. That is why you have me."

CHAPTER 18

[Farfariello's] appeal is made directly to the very people he
characterizes or caricatures. Almost every one of his types is present
in his audiences every night, and they have some appreciation
for the care he devotes to his impersonations, the reverence he
feels for his art. His reward is complete understanding, a wave
of personal feeling that destroys the barrier of the footlights.
It is a reward which is bestowed on few interpreters.
—Carl Van Vechten, theater critic

As he did every evening of his day off, Paolo stood on Sixth Avenue,
between Forty-Third and Forty-Fourth, and gazed up at the red brick
and terra-cotta beaux-arts building with its white accents and Moorish
corner towers, topped with a framework of iron globes. About the time

the electric lights were lit on each of the four spheres, Luisa, daughter of the up-and-coming attorney Guido Morosco, would appear, take his hand, and share the inspiring view a moment longer. By now, their shipboard romance was in full flourish. But as had been the case for more than a year, their trysts were cloaked in secrecy. Signore Morosco would never approve of his daughter carrying on with the likes of a street urchin such as Paolo LaChimia.

Paolo, of course, saw himself differently. His labors for Nicolo Bertolino earned him enough money to dress like a gentleman, eat well, and enjoy some of the finer things his new country had to offer—such as these weekly visits with Luisa to the Hippodrome Theatre, the largest complex of its kind in the world. When the likes of W. G. Stewart, George Wilson, the Leo Davis Troupe, Harry Wordell, and the El Rey Sisters were performing, every one of the 5,300 seats was filled with an enthusiastic patron. The great two-hundred-foot-deep stage had a fourteen-foot-high rising glass water tank, sixty feet in diameter, for the swimming and diving shows. There were circus animals, opulent sets, and a five-hundred-member chorus. This was Paolo's America.

Whenever they visited, he would buy them each some candy and a souvenir program—the one where he had first seen the advertisement for Fatima Sensible Cigarettes that had captured his imagination for his future. In profile was a man in a perfect woolen suit, his hand cradling an open book. The cigarette was carefully pinched between two fingers. Months ago, Paolo had begged Signora Alessi to teach him to read the opening lines: "Not every man of affairs smokes 5 cent Fatimas. They are coming every day to be a standard smoke with more and more clear thinking substantial men."

Standing there with his Fatima, wearing a wry smile and a suit from the wardrobe Signore Bertolino provided, Paolo felt confident.

Luisa touched his arm. "You are a substantial man," she whispered.

"Oh, so the lovely Luisa makes a tease," he said.

"No, Signore LaChimia, only a half tease."

"Come, *carina*, we should take our seats. I don't want to miss one moment of Farfariello," Paolo said as he urged her toward the entrance.

"Ah yes, the king of New York vaudeville," Luisa announced melodramatically.

Paolo frowned.

"Oh, stop, Paolo. I tease again."

Eduardo Migliaccio, inventor of the tragicomic character Farfariello, was Paolo's favorite entertainer. Tonight, this *caratterista* would transform himself through twenty or more roles, convoluting the language with his Italo-Americanese while parodying greenhorns, opera divas, street cleaners, bootleggers, and more. Migliaccio had perfected the *cafone*, who adopted the mannerisms, clothes, and slang of this country but in actuality was no more American than the day he disembarked. Ironically, his repertoire of over 150 sketches helped ease the tensions and anxieties of assimilation.

The evening started in relatively mundane fashion, with Migliaccio's powerful baritone belting out a song. But then he disappeared into the wings. The chatter grew louder in the smoky theater, the audience anticipating the first impersonation. In minutes, he reemerged as a French concert hall soubrette, complete with extraordinarily large buttocks and bosom. And then, at a rapid-fire pace, he was an Italian patriot with a mustache and tricolor Italian sash, a Spanish dancer, a funeral director, a bootlegger, a gangster, and a fireman. With each scene, the calls for "ice man" grew louder. Finally, he returned, as he always did, to complete his night as the folk song–singing ice man. As he took to the stage again, Paolo and Luisa stood and cheered with five thousand other souls and then settled reverently in their seats to hear the songs that suggested both their homeland and their adopted country.

Luisa squeezed Paolo's hand. She pretended not to see the pools that were forming in his eyes. Migliaccio's ice man had that effect on him.

But it was the same for a thousand immigrants at the Hippodrome that night, who had one foot in their adopted country and the other still on the cobblestone street of some remote village in Mezzogiorno. Farfariello had an uncanny way of pressing a finger into the wound of their conflict. Remarkable opportunity came at a price. They all knew that. It was the profound sadness that had been unexpected.

Once out onto Forty-Third, Paolo was able to recover, press his lips to Fatima's, and regain his advantage over melancholy.

"I think it is time, Paolo," Luisa said.

"Time?" he questioned.

"My father is home. By now he has poured his third glass of Barolo. Please, Paolo."

"You think the wine will change his disposition? Come close, Luisa."

She leaned in.

"The *nebbiolo* grape produces a wine that is both powerful and elegant. The elegance, he passed on to you. The power, he retains."

Luisa looked at him curiously. She did not understand.

"With a belly full of Barolo, he will kill me."

"You can't avoid him forever," she said, pouting.

"Luisa, I've spent my life learning to be a ghost. I could live in his house, and he would never see me."

Luisa smiled.

"No, you troublemaker," Paolo said, feigning anger.

The trip back to Luisa's flat was always an adventure. To save cab fare, they walked much of it, sometimes along Sixth, sometimes Seventh. They often zigzagged their way through side streets. In this way, Paolo could accomplish two things: first, more time with Luisa and more stolen kisses along backstreets and second, a geography lesson. In his work for Signore Bertolino, Paolo needed to know the streets.

At Gramercy Park, their legs would give out, and Paolo would hail a cab for the last third of the trip. They would almost always disembark at Barclay and Church, on the south end of City Hall Park, where they would share one long, last embrace before Luisa walked the short distance back to Beekman. From this corner, Paolo could watch after her until she disappeared into her family's walk-up.

Paolo would then continue his journey southeast toward Cuyler's Alley. As he did following every visit to the Hippodrome, he would recount the performances and imagine himself on that massive stage. On this particular evening he fancied himself as the show's *cafone*, a bouncer on Mulberry Street daydreaming of moving his profession to Broadway, surrounded by furs and fast cars.

"*O Supuorto e Mulberry Stritto*," he announced aloud. He continued, "But what a fool I am. Here I stand on Mulberry Stritto, day and night, as if there existed in Nuovo Yorca only this street and nothing more. At Brodaway they value you when you walk with a stick."

When he arrived at the barber shop, the lights were still on. Signore Bertolino often met late into the night with his employees, so Paolo expected to find the usual cast of characters—and the usual exchange of envelopes. But when he walked in, only Nicolo Bertolino and Signora Alessi were there. A lump formed in Paolo's throat. Something wasn't right.

"Welcome, home, Paolo," Bertolino said. "Signora Alessi and I were just talking about you."

"Is something wrong, signore?" Paolo asked.

"Absolutely not. Something is very right," a voice called out from the shadows. Signore Fabbiano stepped into the light.

Paolo's heart sank. He hadn't seen Fabbiano in more than a year. For a couple of days after dropping Paolo off at the barber shop, Fabbiano had come and gone, but he had then disappeared.

"Signore Fabbiano," Paolo stuttered.

"Come now, signore," Fabbiano said with a smile. "It is a reunion, no? Then greet me properly." He pulled Paolo to him and kissed each of his cheeks, catching Paolo off guard. "Bertolino tells me wonderful things about your studies. You have become the star pupil at L'Academia Fabbiano!" Fabbiano laughed. "Signora, you do exceptional work."

"I love America," Paolo said a bit too loudly. He suddenly felt as though he were defending his place here. Fabbiano represented the boat. That was all Paolo knew. And he was not about to return to it.

"What is not to love, Paolo?" Fabbiano said. "When I am away on business, it is all I think about."

"And Signore Fabbiano and I believe you are planting some very profitable seeds in our adopted country," Nicolo Bertolino added.

"Seeds?" Paolo was unsure what he meant.

"You are making friends, no?" Fabbiano asked.

"Yes, some," Paolo answered hesitantly.

"And the lovely Luisa Morosco?" Fabbiano asked.

"Signore Bertolino, today was my day off," Paolo protested.

"*E vero*, Paolo," Bertolino said. "It is true. No one is questioning you. In fact, Signore Fabbiano is very impressed."

Paolo frowned.

"Guido Morosco has, in very short order, become the city's most prominent immigration attorney," Fabbiano stated. "He has won hundreds of cases for his clients. We have much to thank him for."

"Do you need his services, signore?" Paolo asked.

"We need *your* services, Paolo," Fabbiano answered.

"But I do not know Signore Morosco," Paolo said. "In fact, I have hidden from him all these months."

"But he knows who you are, Paolo," Bertolino said. "Believe me, he knows who you are. You will go to him."

"For what, signore?" Paolo argued. "You can call his secretary. Make an appointment."

"Paolo!" Signora Alessi scolded. "You do not talk to Signore that way. You will do what he asks."

"I did not mean any disrespect, signore," Paolo said.

"Look, Signorino Paolo," Fabbiano said sternly. "You are a smart young man. Claudio spotted that on the *Santa Ana* before Naples disappeared from the horizon. In Palermo you made a living by charming lire away from unsuspecting souls. You have now won the favor of Guido Morosco's only daughter. That is not something to be taken lightly. It is something we must exploit. And you will do precisely as Bertolino instructs. Do I make myself clear?"

"Yes, Signore Fabbiano," Paolo answered. "Forgive me."

"Very good," Fabbiano said. "Now leave us. Get some sleep. Tomorrow you will add Signore Morosco to your list of clients. And we will begin our new relationship with him."

"Tomorrow?" Paolo questioned.

"Good night, Paolo," Signora Alessi insisted.

"Good night," Paolo said, and he reluctantly headed for the stairway.

"Wear the blue pinstripe tomorrow," Bertolino called after him. "When you face a lawyer, you must look like one."

CHAPTER 19

Bring me the sunflower so I can transplant it
to my earth scorched with salt,
so it can display all day to the azure mirrors
of sky the anxiety of its yellow face.

Dark things stretch towards brightness,
bodies exhaust themselves in a flow
of colours: this in music. To vanish
is thus the hazard of venturing.
—Eugenio Montale, "Bring Me the Sunflower"

October 1917

With the declaration of war on Germany and the subsequent Selective Service Act, signed into law at the start of Woodrow Wilson's second term, the American landscape was once again changing for the already-confused Italian immigrant population. Back at home, Prime Minister Salandra, despite disapproval by the overwhelming majority in Parliament, had decided it was in Italy's best interest to enter the war. So now the Italians' home country was battling Austria-Hungary in its own war along its northern border. Harsh winters, treacherous terrain, and little or no supplies were taking a toll on the Italian troops.

Stefano Mosca, eldest son of Giuseppe and Marianna, had left his home, his mother, and his sister Adelina the year before to join his comrades in arms. In the months before enlisting, Stefano had argued incessantly with Marianna, dismissed his ailing sibling, and cursed his father for leaving the motherland. And then one day he simply had not come home. Marianna and Adelina were left alone as Adelina's condition worsened.

Marianna had been faithful in her monthly letters to her husband, so Giuseppe knew of his son's departure. He suspected that Stefano had been lured by some misguided romantic notion of war and victory for the common man.

What Giuseppe did not know was that Stefano and several hundred thousand other Italian troops were suffering through eleven battles along the Ilonzo River. The last one would take place at Caporetto, in the valley of Mount Nero, in the eastern sector of the Italian front. There the enemy would virtually destroy the Italian Second Army, capturing 275,000 and killing nearly 150,000 more, but Stefano would manage to escape and make his way south to Milano.

Giuseppe spent many a sleepless night worrying about his beloved wife and their frail eleven-year-old daughter. In two years, he had been unable to send home the funds he had hoped. But finally, with the help of Bernard Ulmann, Giuseppe was opening his own modest tailor shop. And on this cool evening, he and Franco, now fourteen, sat on the stoop outside the one-room store as a carpenter hammered away at some shelving inside.

"Papa, what are you thinking about?" Franco asked. "You are staring, but you look at nothing."

"Amarelli *liquirizia*," Giuseppe answered.

"That is awful stuff," Franco said with a frown.

Giuseppe smiled as he chewed on a licorice root. Next to him was a small paper sack filled with roots and tiny, black, anise-flavored pieces he would occasionally toss into his mouth as well.

"Papa, you look funny. Your lips are black."

"I have Calabria on my face," Giuseppe laughed. "Amarelli makes the very best licorice in all the world, in the Cosenza province, not far from Mama and Adelina. Signore Cuomo brought this back with him, and I talked him out of a bag for us."

"For you," Franco corrected.

"*E quasi ora*, Franco," Giuseppe said.

"Use your English, Papa," Franco scolded.

"Almost … it is time," Giuseppe said, struggling with the translation.

"Time for what?" Franco asked.

"*Lunedi* …" Giuseppe began, reverting again to Italian.

"Papa," Franco interjected in an admonishing tone.

"*Va bene* … on Monday," he said, "I send the last money for Mama *e* Adelina."

"They are coming?" Franco shouted.

"Very soon. Very soon, my son."

"Oh, Papa, that is such good news!" Franco exclaimed. "We must get the flat ready."

"Today, *la festa*. Tomorrow we will clean out that storage room next to the kitchen," Giuseppe said.

"You can't put Mama there," Franco argued.

"*Sei un buffone*," Giuseppe laughed. "The room will be for you. Mama will sleep with me, of course." He let that sink in a moment.

"And look," Giuseppe said as he reached for something in his inside jacket pocket. He struggled to remove a large, nearly mangled, folded envelope. He placed it on his lap and looked at it as though admiring something very precious.

"What is it, Papa? Let me see."

He unwrapped the paper and gently lifted out a filet-lace doily.

"Mama's lace?" Franco asked. "I don't understand."

"But she will," Giuseppe said with a smile. "She will."

For the next several minutes the two sat in silence, each one imagining the day when Marianna and Adelina would step onto Ellis Island and join them.

Giuseppe looked out onto a world in transition. He wondered how his wife would respond to this tangled city. The streets were filled with horse-drawn carriages and carts, trollies, elevated trains, and gasoline-powered automobiles. And in the midst of all of the turmoil, the streets themselves teemed with dodging pedestrians, as though no sidewalks existed at all. This chaos was many worlds away from the mountains of Serra San Bruno.

There were familiar signs, of course—an Italian band here; a puppet show there; men at makeshift tables, sipping wine and playing *mora*, *briscola*, and *tresette*. Around the corner was a coffee house where dialect plays were performed. And today was *la festa*. Oh, how he wished Marianna could arrive on a day like today. After all, they had met on such a day, at *la festa* in Pizzoni, her hometown.

But this *festa* was one Italians in America claimed for themselves—the Feast of San Gennaro. On this day, the men of the Church of the Most Precious Blood would hoist the statue of San Gennaro on their shoulders and march through the streets of Little Italy. There would be parades and music and marionettes and the smell of roasted chestnuts and *braciole*.

As the procession wound along the length of Mulberry and Mott Streets, between Canal and Houston, Giuseppe and Franco clapped and laughed. When San Gennaro passed by, Franco's father gave him some money to pin to the statue. They quietly prayed for Marianna and Adelina to come to them soon.

"Franco," Giuseppe yelled over the music, "San Gennaro will bring them! He was martyred for the faith. He will hear us in heaven." A moment later, Giuseppe, exclaimed, "Look, Franco! *Il Sono a Ballu!*"

Franco clapped for the troupe of female performers who stopped in front of them. Flutes, fiddles, trumpets, mandolins, accordions, and of course, the *zampogna* were played in 6/8 time while the women, dressed in traditional Calabrian garb, danced frantically. It was the tarantella, and it immediately transported both Giuseppe and Franco back to Serra San Bruno. The women portrayed victims of the poisonous bite of the spider. In an attempt to drive the venom out, they would dance to exhaustion.

"Signore Mosca," a voice called from behind them. "Signore Mosca?"

Giuseppe turned and stood to face a well-dressed gentleman accompanied by a young girl. "Can I help you, signore?" Giuseppe asked.

"I am sorry to interrupt the *festa*, but I was told I could find you here today," the gentleman said apologetically.

"No, it is fine. I work every day. We were just watching the parade," Giuseppe said.

"I am Guido Morosco. This is my daughter, Luisa."

Franco extended his hand to Luisa. "I am Franco Mosca," he said.

She condescendingly touched his cheek. "Such a sweet boy," she said.

"How can I help you, signore?" Giuseppe asked.

"Well," Guido said, unfurling a catalogue, "I was hoping you could make me some suits like the ones in this book."

Giuseppe took the catalogue from Guido, briefly leafed through some pages, and handed it over to Franco.

"*The Style Book for Men and Young Men*," Franco read aloud. "Fall 1917. Hart, Schaffner, and Marx."

"And why are you not buying from this … place?" Giuseppe asked.

"There are three reasons, signore," Guido said. "First, I have seen your work. Such artistry I have not witnessed since leaving Naples. Second, I am in the business of supporting Italians who, like me, have made their home here. And third, these are Germans."

"Franco," Giuseppe said, pointing to a page in the catalogue, "what do those words say? Right there below the picture."

"Insist on all wool," Franco read slowly. "It is more important than ever to be careful. Woolen fabrics give longer service and fit better."

"They mix it with cotton. They cheapen," Giuseppe said.

"See?" Guido said. "I come to the master."

"I can make, of course," Giuseppe responded. "You like the new military look these days? The pockets, the waist, the brass buttons?"

"Precisely," Guido said.

"You can come tomorrow?" Giuseppe asked. "I have a man inside who is making much sawdust."

"Yes. First thing."

"*Va bene*, signore," Giuseppe said. "And thank you."

"No. Thank you," Guido said as he took Luisa's hand and turned to leave.

Luisa glanced back at Franco and smiled. Franco awkwardly turned away.

Giuseppe grabbed Franco by the neck and laughed. "You like the girl, Franco?"

"Stop it, Papa," he said, pulling away. "She will see."

"Then she will see this as well," Giuseppe announced, and he planted a kiss on his son's cheek.

"Papa!"

As they turned to go inside the shop, a young man called out. "Mister, mister!"

"I am open tomorrow." Giuseppe waved his hand without looking and continued inside.

"No," the young man protested.

Giuseppe and Franco turned to find a boy of no more than twelve, dressed in a blue shirt and matching cap with the word "Messenger" embroidered across the front.

"Then what is it?" Giuseppe asked.

"I am looking for a Guy … sa … pee … pee," the boy said, struggling to read the name on an envelope he carried.

"There is no one here with that name," Giuseppe answered.

"No, Papa," Franco said, looking at the envelope, "he means you. Giuseppe Mosca, it says."

"Western Union," the boy clarified. "I have a telegram."

"Franco," Giuseppe ordered, "read it. What does it say? Is it from Mama? But she should not be so extravagant … A telegram? Perhaps she has made arrangements to come."

The boy handed the envelope to Franco, who unfolded the contents—a single yellow paper—and began reading aloud. "The Western Union Telegraph Company. Twenty-three thousand offices in America. Cable services to all the world."

"Yes, yes, yes, but what does it say?" Giuseppe asked impatiently.

"My dearest husband," Franco continued, "I am sorry to tell you from such a distance. On Friday, our sweet Adelina went to be with the Lord … Papa!"

CHAPTER 20

For all of their wisdom, none of the Italian immigrant parents I knew grasped the dilemma of their children, who, from early childhood, were pulled in one direction by their parents' insistence on old world traditions and in the opposite direction by what their teachers told them in the classroom. In this inadvertent tug of war, the parents often prevailed, and the children were left with confused impressions of identity that were never resolved. I resolved mine by becoming an ethnic at large, with one foot in my Sicilian heritage, the other in the American mainstream. By this cultural gymnastic stance I could derive strength from my past and a feeling of hope for my present.
—Jerre Mangione, *An Ethnic at Large*

D espite his uncle's insistence that "Americanization" would move Aldo's career along more rapidly, Joseph Carabelli continued to promote Aldo at a steady pace. It certainly didn't hurt that the inventory of competition had been depleted throughout the end of 1917 and well into 1918. The Great War and Wilson's selective service had seen to that. Still, Aldo Grimaldi's talents were undeniable. His fresco and mosaic work, in particular, were something to behold. And he had that rare ability to get more out of a crew than most of his contemporaries. Carabelli recognized that and rewarded him with management responsibilities and better pay.

They were more than three years removed from the *Santa Ana* now, and Anna had convinced Aldo that they should try to provide a brother or sister for Salvatore. Anna was now eight months pregnant, but her routine remained just as energetic as before. She rose early each morning to ensure Aldo was properly dressed and fed, walked Salvatore to school, attended mass, and then spent the day organizing fundraising opportunities for their parish.

On November 11, 1918, the very same day Anna gave birth to Maria, Germany surrendered, and all nations agreed to a cease-fire. There were great celebrations, but Aldo, a skeptic by nature, did not trust what he called an informal peace. At the moment, though, he was more concerned for his family's health. Influenza, which had begun its penetration into Cleveland in late September, was now being declared an epidemic by the city health commissioner, Dr. Harry Rockwood. By mid-October, schools had closed, church services had been suspended, and virtually every venue of public gathering had been declared off-limits.

Aldo's hours actually increased as a number of laborers fell ill. Anna worried for his safety. "You must consider staying indoors, Aldo," she insisted.

"Indoors? Are you serious, Anna? And what will we eat? Our shoes?"

By the time the crisis had passed in March 1919, almost 24,000 Clevelanders had contracted the illness, and more than 3,600 had succumbed. Fortunately, the Grimaldis and the Michelis had not come down with so much as a sniffle. Salvatore returned to school, the Ginney Block was once again alive with activity, and Anna resumed her volunteer efforts at church, with four- month old Maria on her hip. She added the daily rosary she had promised *il Signore* if He spared them.

Finally, on June 28, 1919, Germany signed the Treaty of Versailles with the Allied nations, including Britain, France, Russia, and Italy. The signing was more symbolic than anything else, since fighting had stopped nearly eight months earlier, but Aldo felt a bit more optimistic about their future.

By 1920, Cleveland had become the fifth-largest city in the United States. Prosperity was returning. For Aldo and his uncle, that meant numerous opportunities as newer, larger structures began to rise in the city.

Salvatore was turning fifteen. His predilection to the physics of structures often had him buried in his favorite publication: the Standard Homes Company's "Better Homes at Lower Cost." He studied the plans and photographs of each of the seventy-seven designs over and over and over again. He carefully considered each wood, brick, stucco and stone edifice. He measured and re-measured each floor plan. And what he didn't understand, he had his father and uncle and cousins to query.

Anna was pregnant again. And even though Maria's birth was physically uneventful, she still worried, given her miscarriage on the Santa Ana five years earlier. Her routine was the same as it was with Maria. In spite of the fact that the odds of losing a child in the last trimester were quite low, she would not even think of buying a single new baby item or preparing additional space for a third child. That would have to come after the birth.

"It is time, nephew," Roberto would repeat at the end of each meal they shared on Sundays.

"Time for what, Uncle?" Aldo would sigh, knowing fully what was coming next.

"Grimaldi and Micheli," Roberto would announce, as if for the first time.

"Signore Carabelli has been good to us," Aldo would protest.

But on one particular Sunday afternoon, Roberto was a bit more resolute.

"I brought you here—not to chip stone in the middle of a cloud of dust, not to bow to the whims of the Carabellis for a fraction of what you are worth. You are carving headstones when you could be building masterpieces."

"You don't know what you are talking about," Aldo said, dismissing his uncle.

"You will respect your elder!" Roberto suddenly fumed. "I know what I am talking about. You do not. You are an artist, but you are a child. Listen to me. This city is waiting for you—for us. There may never be a better time than now."

"You know, Robert," Aldo practically spat, "you left Napoli as a proud Italian. You spoke the language of your ancestors. You ate our food. You followed our traditions. But now you've come to this L'America, and I can't tell you apart from the Irish or the Germans or the Slavs. Your wife wears their clothes. Your sons talk their words. And I am supposed to respect that? Your brother, my father, is rolling over in his grave."

Salvatore, who had been listening to the radio with his cousins in another room, suddenly burst into the dining room, followed by Gianni and Carlo.

"They won!" Salvatore exclaimed. "The Indians won the World Series! Five games to two. The Dodgers were nothing! They couldn't stay on the field with Tris Speaker's Cleveland Indians!"

"Again with the baseball. See? You even turn my son," Aldo lamented.

Roberto laughed. "Nephew, it's not much, but Teresa and I, with the help of the boys, have been able to put some money in the bank."

"Uncle Roberto—" Aldo started.

"Look at your wife. *Sta andando per splodere.* She is going to explode. In two months, you will have your third child. Your pride is not going to educate them. This city needs us. Think about it—my knowledge, your talent. *E perfetto.*"

"And I am going to be your architect, Papa," Salvatore exclaimed.

Aldo smiled. "So you say. So you always say, my young engineer."

When Aldo returned to work the following morning, there was a message that Mr. Carabelli needed to see him before he started the day. Carabelli never summoned him. Aldo started recounting his last several projects. Was there a problem with the Richards family headstone? The civic monument honoring Clevelanders who had died in the Great War?

Aldo downed his morning espresso, took a deep breath, and approached Joseph Carabelli's office. The door was slightly open, and Aldo could see Carabelli and a young man he did not recognize. They were laughing. Aldo was encouraged. You don't laugh just before you fire someone.

"Aldo," Carabelli said, motioning with his hand, "come in, come in. Don't stand out there eavesdropping."

"Eaves?" Aldo asked as he entered the room. "What is—?"

"Never mind," Carabelli said. "I want you to meet someone. Say hello to John Johns."

Aldo reached out his hand.

"Yes, you heard right," John said. "I have two first names. My parents aren't very imaginative."

"John is fresh out of architecture school," Carabelli explained. "The son of a very close friend. Very talented young man. He's going to be a valuable asset to our firm."

"Asset?" Aldo was confused.

"Today's his first day. I want you to teach him everything you know. Show him the ropes. He'll pick things up very quickly. You'll see. One of these days he'll be bossing us around," Carabelli laughed. "Aldo's my best stonecutter."

"I do more than cut stone, Mr. John. There is much more," Aldo said slowly.

"Of course, of course," Carabelli said dismissively. "John, I want you to shadow Aldo—on everything, from picking out granite and marble to how he handles a rocko and tooth chisel. Hell, if he goes to the washroom to relieve himself, I want you to watch how he shakes it." Carabelli laughed even louder than before.

"Mr. Carabelli has told me so much about you," John said. "I look forward to getting to know you."

"Yes, yes," Carabelli said, waving at the two men. "Off with you now. John, come back and see me at the end of the day. Elizabeth is planning a beautiful meal this evening. Wait till you taste her *pasta con carciofi*. No one can make an artichoke sing like my Elizabeth."

CHAPTER 21

Cannery Row in Monterey in California is a poem, a stink, a grating
noise, a quality of light, a tone, a habit, a nostalgia, a dream. Cannery
Row is the gathered and scattered, tin and iron and rust and splintered
wood, chipped pavement and weedy lots and junk heaps, sardine
canneries of corrugated iron, honky tonks, restaurants and whore
houses, and little crowded groceries, and laboratories and flophouses.
—John Steinbeck, *Cannery Row*

August 1921

Paolo awoke midafternoon to the sound of competing gulls and street
vendors. The sour salt air was all too familiar. He had sworn that he'd
never again subject himself to the overnight forages, and yet here he was,

keeping odd hours and wiping the sleep out of his eyes with hands reeking of a life he thought he had discarded in Sicily.

It had been several months, but he felt as though the sting of Signora Alessi's slap still resonated. "How dare you!" she had screamed. "Signore Bertolino gave you everything. Everything! *Te diede vita in questo paese.* He gave you life in L'America. And you sneak away in the middle of the night like a thief."

Paolo had suppressed a smirk, given his colleagues and circumstances. But it was true. The moment they had insisted he strong-arm Luisa's father, he knew he had to leave—and not just Bertolino's shop. He would have to go a considerable distance to escape the formidable reach of his mentor. Paolo's uncle's house in Monterey, California, was about as far away as he could imagine. So he had gathered up his savings, along with his paper valise that had somehow survived the passage from Italy, and quietly descended the back stairs when he was certain no one was awake.

He hadn't counted on Alessi's heartburn. He hadn't seen her in the shadows until her fist was full of his shirt.

"Signora! You scared me!" he had wailed.

There was no arguing his point. He decided to take all she was giving him, which was considerable. And when she was finished—when her lecture was over, when she had slapped him—she grabbed the back of his neck and pulled him close to her, so close that her ample breasts pressed hard against his face. She held him there for what seemed minutes. When she pushed him away, he could see her red eyes awash in tears. Drop after drop coursed down the deep ridges on her face that had formed after years of service to Bertolino.

"*Mi dispiace*" was all Paolo could manage.

"In English," she demanded.

"I am sorry."

"Go … wherever it is, go. But it must be far, or the next time I see you, it will be in a box."

Signora Alessi had then turned and slipped into the darkness. Paolo had waited a moment and then pushed outside into the chill of predawn New York City.

Paolo hadn't counted on just how far away California was. He hadn't expected his journey to take nearly twice as long as the trip on the *Santa Ana*. He hadn't been prepared for the trains and buses and long hours waiting in cold stations. But now here he was.

Zio Gregorio LaChimia had been overwhelmed to see him—family from Palermo, a talented nephew with net-mending ability and knowledge of the trade. Especially now that the sardines were running in great numbers, this was a gift from God.

"When was the last time you fished?" Gregorio asked.

"About five years ago. Mackerel and anchovies."

"Lampara nets?" Gregorio asked in anticipation.

"That's all we used," Paolo answered.

"Wonderful. A gift from God," Gregorio said, making the sign of the cross. "But we fish sardines. No quarter oils."

Paolo frowned.

"It's a term we use for smaller fish. The canneries, they want the six- to eight-packs. You make the mesh to hold them and let the quarter oils go. And wait till you see what Pietro Ferrante did to the nets. He made some wonderful changes—wings. They work better than ever in this bay. The Chinese and Portuguese used to own these waters. Not today. Today it's the Sicilians. We put those bastards in the canneries. Now they cut our fish." He laughed as he hugged Paolo.

"Pietro Ferrante?" Paolo asked.

"The king of sardines in Monterey. He built the San Carlos cannery. He's one of us. He's from Isola della Femmine, just like Giuseppe DiMaggio. I'll introduce you to them all," Gregorio bellowed.

When Paolo first arrived, he wasn't sure what his uncle cared more for—him or the damned sardines. But he soon learned that Gregorio had a passion for both his work and his family. He was childless, and since the death of his wife, the sardines had been winning much more favor.

Paolo headed away from their small house on Clay Street, in the heart of Spaghetti Hill, and turned down West Franklin and then Pacific Street, toward Pacific Steamship Wharf. One block east was Lake El Estero, a quiet palm-lined spot that reminded him of Palermo. He would often stop along the gentle slope, as he did this day, and look out onto the bay. To the west was the Southern Pacific train station, where he had arrived some months earlier. Beyond that, the waters were peppered with mostly lampara boats, twenty to thirty feet long, high-bowed with rounded sterns. Here, they were usually made of Douglas fir and redwood. Most were joined to smaller open wooden barges, called lighters. These were used to haul the catch to the canneries.

Before making his way down to the docks, Paolo glanced back up the hill, as he always did. This time of year, he was learning, there was a confusion of color—bluish-green bishop pines, dotted with their maroon cone clusters; sycamores; golden cottonwoods; orange-red liquidambars; purple leaf plumbs; and of course, the burgundy and bronze vineyards.

But today, he did not linger. Last night, the catch had been huge, but on the last cast, the net had suffered under the weight of a sea lion. At least six or eight feet near the cork line had been shredded as the creature fought to free itself. Paolo needed to locate the breach on the 1,200-foot net, repair it, and pile it on the launch to be ready for sundown. Nighttime—that was when the most curious hunt, at least to California newcomer Paolo, would begin.

At nightfall, the US Navy Air Station would dispatch a navy pilot and crew trained to locate sardines, who swam near the surface of the waves. At night, especially during the dark of the moon, they would look for that bright crescent of light the school gave off. Its unmistakable inner edge was green, and the outer edge was red. That's when the plane would signal a Coast Guard cutter nearby, which in turn would inform a fleet of fishing vessels standing at the ready. And the chase was on.

Crews on boats ranging in size from twenty feet to sixty-five feet would race to the location, man their nets, and embark on a frenzy of activity until the catch was complete. Most employed the lampara nets—a surrounding net in the shape of a spoon with a short lead line under a much longer float line. There was a central bunt to contain the fish and lateral wings used for hauling it in.

With his thirty-foot lampara boat and accompanying lighter, Gregorio had to work quickly and efficiently to deliver his haul to the cannery and head out for more. The sixty-five-foot purse-seine boats, with their mechanical nets on turntables, could easily out fish him. But Gregorio was known for his tireless efforts and multiple hauls. His crew of five always slept well just after dawn.

Activity was just as frenetic onshore at the canneries. They stood as far out from the rocky coast as possible to enable the boats to easily maneuver into position. Whistles would blow signaling a delivery, and that's when the boilers were fired, and the on-call laborers had forty-five minutes to get to their work stations. All night long, the scene repeated itself. At one end, whole sardines were dumped onto conveyors. On the other end were warehouses where railroad freight cars delivered cans and supplies and pulled out with cased sardines, fishmeal, and sardine oil. The entire town of Monterey stank of fish, but the locals were fond of calling it "the smell of success."

As the sun began to appear above Spaghetti Hill, Paolo struggled to begin his walk home. Tonight they had had three hauls, each at about sixty tons. This was so much harder than separating unsuspecting tourists from wallets and watches. Paolo had often considered utilizing his considerable skills on the people who frequented Cannery Row, but this month with Uncle Gregorio had begun to change him somehow. He felt more principled. These were his colleagues. It was strange territory for a young man who not so very long ago had aspired to Cosa Nostra hierarchy.

"Nephew," Gregorio called to him. "Join us for some grappa. You earned it tonight."

"No, thank you, Zio," Paolo sighed. "I'm much too tired."

"Oh, these youngsters today. No energy. They wilt so fast," Gregorio said, laughing with his friends.

Then, as they did almost every morning after a catch, Gregorio and his mates sat around some broken lobster crates, downed their precious grappa, and recounted the night or told tall tales or argued over the best way to cook octopus.

"No, no, no … *lei idiote sanno niente.* You idiots know nothing," Giuseppe DiMaggio roared. "After the salty water boils, you dip the octopus into it, then pull it out. Dip again and pull out. Then one more time. Only then do you let it settle to the bottom. Twenty minutes—no more. Then let it cool. And don't touch! The fish will tense up and get tough. Don't laugh. It is true. Trust me. This way is tender, *al dente.*"

Once home, Paolo settled himself at the little table next to his bed. As he did almost every day after work, he began to write English words on the pad beside the lamp. He was determined to learn this blasted language. And perhaps today would be the day he sent the letter. He turned over the page and began to write: "My dearest Luisa, I am sorry for no telling you about this travels."

CHAPTER 22

"In the Italian borders,
Italians have been remade
Mussolini has remade them
For tomorrow's war,
For labor's glory,
For peace and for the laurel,
For the shame of those
Who repudiated our Fatherland."
—Salvatore Gotta, "Giovinezza"

November 1925

G iuseppe Mosca sat with a half smile as read his copy of *L'Italo-Americano*. Franco, now twenty, had been tutoring his father in English every week for the past four years. His lessons included reading in Italian as well. There were a lot of words Giuseppe still did not know, but he was finally able to understand and get by. The fire was bright, but the voices and smells from the kitchen were what truly warmed him this evening. His Marianna had at long last been able to join them several years ago. He had made good on his promise to make a place for her. In fact, he now felt guilty paying the eighteen dollars per month for their five-room flat above the new store on Mulberry. It wasn't that he wanted to deprive Marianna of anything, but he watched as the less fortunate struggled daily to survive. And of course, he remembered the rags and the bones.

As soon as she arrived, the man Giuseppe regarded as his *angelo custode*, his guardian angel, Bernard Ulmann, had offered her a job at Ullmann and Company/Bucilla. Her needlepoint skills were a natural fit for the knitting and embroidery supply company. Marianna believed that San Bruno was responsible for her fortuity. She had felt this especially when Ulmann decided in 1922 to create one of the earliest forms of an employee stock ownership plan. He encouraged Giuseppe and Marianna to participate when he sold Bucilla to the employees. He took an extraordinary amount of time to explain the opportunity to them both. Giuseppe had an unreserved belief in Ulmann, so they made the purchase, and over the last few years, Franco had often reminded them of the wisdom of that.

"Marianna, listen to this!" Giuseppe called out to her. "Some *patso matto* in Roma—what is his name, Tito Zaniboni—tried to shoot *Il Duce* earlier this month. He had a rifle at Palazzo Chigi. The police, though— they caught him before."

"Maybe it is not so bad a thing, Babo," she said. "Mussolini scares me."

"*Il Fascisti?*" he asked. "Do you see what the party is doing? He drained the swamps to deliver water to the crops. He builds the power plants. And great highways."

"Where was our water in Serra?" she asked. "Maybe you want to buy a motorcar and drive it on his autostrada."

"That is not the point, Marianna. I am happy for the people we left behind."

Marianna fingered the note in her apron pocket, one of several she had withheld from her husband. "Left behind," she mumbled under her breath.

"Papa, don't be so quick to pin a medal on your Mussolini," Franco said as he poked his head in from the kitchen. "I am not so sure our beloved Calabria is enjoying his bounty."

"What happened to the little boy in short pants who regarded every word I spoke?" Giuseppe retorted. "You are a big shot now with your own opinions. Does this impress the lovely Luisa?"

"As a matter of fact, it does," Luisa said as she stepped into view and put her arms around Franco.

Luisa Morosco, daughter of Giuseppe's greatest client and advocate, Guido, had become Franco's constant companion. She had matured into a beautiful, confident, and educated young woman. Following in her father's footsteps, she had earned her law degree and was working in his firm, specializing in immigration issues. She still retained her edge and was quick to enter any debate, but the Moscas adored her and the influence she had on their son.

Franco's keen interest in mathematics had led him to seek a career in accounting. President Coolidge had signed into law the Revenue Act in 1924, giving Franco's CPA status official recognition as a professional designation. Giuseppe was so proud. That was yet another excuse to celebrate, which the Mosca patriarch was so fond of doing. And tonight was no different. Giuseppe insisted the family celebrate their tenth year in America and Mosca Tailoring's eighth anniversary.

So celebrate they did, around a table of *abbondanza incredibile e amore*. Calabrese loved their antipasti, so every square inch of cloth was covered with the delicacies. There was *caviole dei poveri*, poor people's caviar. It was nothing more than pickled herring roe in oil, flavored with hot peppers, but Giuseppe considered it the food of royalty. There was bread smeared with *nduja*, a spreadable pork sausage, a favorite from the town of Spilinga in Giuseppe's beloved Vibo Valentia. There were plenty of olives and chicory in oil and vinegar, ripe cheeses, pickled artichoke hearts, and finocchio, the aromatic fennel that reminded Giuseppe of Zia Annunziata, whom he toasted on every occasion.

"Zia sold her donkey to do this thing for us. I ask God for forgiveness every day for how I hated her for interfering. But Zia knew what was best, God rest her soul," he said as he lifted his wine glass.

And then came the pasta—*fileia*. They were short lengths, rolled around sticks to create narrow pipes, and served with a pork, veal, and goat meat sauce that was a specialty of Marianna's.

"Mama, it's the best I've ever tasted," Franco said with a mouthful of *fileia*. "Please pass the *cipolli rosi*," he said, pointing to the bowl of red onions.

"No," Giuseppe insisted. "No more of those onions."

"Babo, we have plenty. Don't be silly," Marianna said.

"It's not that, Marianna. You know why."

"Oh, such an old wives' tale," she laughed.

"What tale?" Luisa asked.

Giuseppe gave his wife a stern look.

"In Calabria, there is a legend about the red onion," said Marianna. "The old people insist it is true." She shook her head.

"We know it to be true, *mi amore*," Giuseppe said with a smile.

"Oh, Babo, not around the children."

"Now I really need to know this," Luisa said as she leaned forward.

"The two of you are still unmarried. It is not right for you to eat *cipolli rosi* together," Giuseppe said authoritatively.

"He thinks they are aphrodisiacs," Marianna scoffed.

The table erupted in laughter.

"Marianna, what do I smell in the kitchen?" Giuseppe asked, trying to change the subject. "Is that what I think it is?"

"*Nzuddo,*" Marianna replied. "I'll get them."

Nzuddo was the Calabrese name for *mastacciolo*, a favorite sweet made of flour, honey, and almonds. Traditionally, they were part of the Feast of Our Lady of Consolation in Reggio Calabria. In the 1500s, Franciscan Capuchins had settled in Reggio, and a wealthy resident had donated a painting by Nicolo Andrea Capriolo to the priests. The painting depicted the Madonna and Child enthroned between Francis of Assisi and Anthony of Padua. For almost four hundred years, on the second Saturday of September, an army of celebrants had been parading the painting from the Basilica of the Hermitage to the cathedral, amid cheers and music and dance.

"You remember, *mi amore?*" Giuseppe asked.

"Of course, Babo," she replied as she placed a huge plate of the treats in the center of the table.

"Remember what?" Luisa asked.

"For our one-year anniversary, my beautiful husband took me to Reggio for the feast—one hundred kilometers from Serra San Bruno to the coast. Until then, the most I had ever traveled was when he brought me the fifteen kilometers from Pizzoni to Serra."

"What a weekend, eh, Marianna?" he said with a wink.

Luisa snickered. "Sounds to me like *cipolli rosi* were involved."

And the table laughed again.

Marianna looked away, and Giuseppe recognized the expression on her face. "Marianna, please. Not tonight."

"There was talk after mass this morning. Maria Allevato heard that he may have come to New York," she said quietly.

"He is dead to me," Giuseppe said flatly.

Marianna reached into her apron pocket. "I have …"

"Dead!" he shouted.

She removed her hand.

◆

In a dark, cold one-room tenement on the East Side, the former Claudia Brumildi paced the threadbare carpet between the single window and a leaky commode. It was almost 2:00 a.m. again. This had become a nightly routine. Each afternoon, without explanation, her unemployed husband would leave the flat after sleeping until noon. She would beg him to look for work. After all, it was he who had insisted they come to L'America shortly after marrying in their tiny village in Italy. It was he who had promised that his passion would find them security and purpose in this new world.

But their relationship had become more and more contentious, and she was feeling like a casualty of his political passion. Now, six months into an unplanned pregnancy, her world had become gray and isolated. The baby needed food, not more pamphlets. And Claudia was suspicious of his comrades, who often showed up and crowded into their tiny room, unannounced and full of rhetoric and cigarettes.

Finally, the door opened, and Stefano Mosca staggered in. He had been drinking again, and he smelled like stale smoke. "Don't ask," he said, raising his hand to her. "You don't understand. Everything I am doing is important for our future—and for the future of our child."

"There will be no future if there is no food, Stefano," Claudia argued.

"Don't be so dramatic. And I have good news."

"What? What good news?" she asked.

"The great man has hired me to be a columnist for *Il Martello*. I will be writing for Carlo Tresca, Claudia. There is no greater honor."

"He's paying you, Stefano? There will be money?" She was trying to stifle her enthusiasm.

"Of course. Look," he said, reaching into his breast pocket. "I have an advance." He showed her several bills. "Enough for coffee and bread in the morning—and after tomorrow's column, some pasta and *vino*," he said with a laugh.

"Oh, Stefano, this is good news indeed." She held him close.

"Claudia, I will be making a difference. I will be part of a new vision, one in which the chasm between the wealthy and poor is closed. Signore Tresca and I will turn the tables on the capitalists who have too long ridden on the backs of downtrodden immigrants in this country. The Fascisti League of North America is gaining strength. They are influencing this misinformed government. You see what they are doing to Tresca and the others—unwarranted arrests, harassment, and now they have influenced your hallowed motherland to revoke our leader's Italian citizenship."

"But I thought we could find our way back home, *amore*," she said, almost in a whisper.

"Home?" he snorted. "There is no home in Italia. This is our home."

"But Mussolini," she implored. "Fascism will return our homeland to what it once was."

"Exactly—a population of backward peasants being led through cow dung by the privileged few. Mussolini is a buffoon, and Fascism is yet another way of suppressing the people."

"Sometimes I don't understand, Stefano. All these words. You don't like Italy, so we come here. And now you don't like America. I am afraid."

"We are here to open eyes, to change this country's misguided admiration of *Il Duce*. The United States claims democracy, but they make love to an ideology like Fascism that is in direct opposition to democracy," he argued.

Claudia was conflicted. She wanted to rejoice over a few dollars, but she feared the cost.

"Now, I must start my column. I'm going to rekindle the fire of Sacco and Vanzetti. We will free them," he announced.

"Oh, Stefano, it is a lost cause. How can you not see that?"

"Stop your infernal criticism!" he suddenly screamed. "You know nothing. You are a stupid pessimist. They have been framed. Listen, do you know the names of the key witnesses at their trial? Do you? Splaine, Devlin, Andrews, Pelzer, Goodrich—Irish, German, and God knows what else. How can you be so blind?"

"Stefano ..."

"You disgust me," he said. "Now make yourself useful and find me some paper."

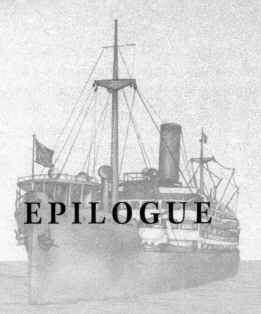

EPILOGUE

August 1927

In the very early morning hours of August 23, much of the eastern half of the United States lay sleeping, while those in the west were preparing to retire. This was not the case for much of the Italian population. Throughout the previous day, word had spread that all attempts to stay the executions of Nicola Sacco and Bartolomeo Vanzetti had failed, and after a six-year-long battle to defend their innocence, electrocutions would finally take place in the minutes following midnight, eastern time.

For several hours, the Grimaldis and Michelis huddled around the radio that Roberto had insisted they purchase in celebration of the contract Grimaldi & Micheli had been awarded to assist in the construction of the Terminal Tower near the Baltimore and Ohio Railroad terminal, just a couple blocks east of the Detroit Superior Bridge. Even Aldo admitted that the large red, white, and green G & M sign that sprawled fifty feet across the eighteenth floor was pretty impressive for both its size and its statement.

The Atwater-Kent Model 37 "modernistic style" radio was the centerpiece of the Micheli living room. The brown wrinkle-finish metal box and matching Type E speaker were prominently displayed on a filet-lace doily atop the mahogany kidney-shaped table, which itself sat beneath a large window that opened onto the front lawn. On hot summer evenings, Aldo and Anna, along with their daughter Maria, now nine, and their son Cristoforo, five, would join their relatives for coffee and dessert as they listened to WJAY broadcast from the Rainbow Room of the Hotel Winton. Their favorite was the Bamboo Garden Orchestra.

But tonight was different. Tonight they awaited word from Charlestown State Prison in Massachusetts. The children had fallen asleep much earlier, but the adults listened for hours as the announcers relived the events that had led up to this night—Sacco and Vanzetti's arrests for the murders of a paymaster and his guard, the circus-like trial, the contradictory testimony. Even the very conservative Aldo had to admit that it appeared as though Sacco and Vanzetti were the poster boys for a growing hatred of Italian socialists and their brand of anarchy. He was convinced that their execution was inevitable and that their spilled blood was considered "necessary" for the atonement of all the immigrants' sins.

Anna quietly prayed the rosary. She believed that *il Signore* would save them. And though he had never been particularly interested in current affairs, she wondered about Salvatore. After graduating from the Knowlton School of Architecture in Columbus, he had taken an internship with C. Howard Crane in that same city, several hours away. He wrote to his parents about his work on the LeVeque Tower, using terms she had to ask Aldo and Roberto to explain.

Roberto now sat on the floor, surrounded by drawings and material lists, pretending to work. Theresa paced back and forth between the living room and the kitchen.

"They should be here," Theresa moaned.

"Who?" Anna asked.

"They have no interest in politics, Ann. You know that," Roberto said.

"She's talking about Carlo and Gianni," Aldo said.

"Carl and John," Roberto said, emphasizing their American names, "are entertaining themselves elsewhere."

"The speakeasy. Always the speakeasy," Theresa lamented.

"I'm sure they have a radio on there. Everyone is listening," Aldo interjected.

———◆———

"Uncle, where are the men? Shouldn't we should be launching?" Paolo asked.

"Tonight, the Portuguese and Asians fish. Let them," Gregorio spat. "And they can drown for all I care," he continued, for anyone within earshot to hear.

"Uncle, you don't mean that," Paolo protested.

"Those poor men are eating their last meal. And for what?" Gregorio asked.

"They were convicted, Uncle—months ago. They admit they are socialists who would do anything for their cause. Murder is not out of the question," Paolo argued.

"*Basta!*" Gregorio shouted. He shook an arthritic finger at Paolo. "How much did you fight to get the life you live? How much? In Palermo you took the money from hardworking people and slept in their beds. You lied your way across the Atlantic Ocean. In New York you were paid to steal. In your entire life, this is the only honest work you have done—a few years, here in this country, with me. And now you are going to spit on Italian brothers who are men enough to stand for something they believe in—not pretend to be something, or someone, else? You don't have the right. You have not earned that right!"

"Uncle, I'm sorry. I didn't realize …"

"Look … look down the line. What do you see?" Gregorio asked.

"Boats," Paolo answered. "All the boats."

"Not all. Just all the Italian boats."

"I see that," Paolo said, nodding.

"That is *una segnale di rispetto*, a sign of respect. Tonight we don't work. We pray for them and their families. We drink to them. We speak their names. They don't even know you, but they are dying for you. You may not agree with them. But they are dying for you."

———————◆———————

Giuseppe and Marianna Mosca made their way through the streets of Greenwich Village, following the directions Franco had reluctantly given them. Franco had wanted to accompany them, but his new wife, the former Luisa Morosco, was suffering through a particularly difficult early pregnancy, and he didn't want to leave her alone.

"Why are we doing this, *mi amore?*" Giuseppe questioned. "Suppose we find him? What then?"

"I am his mother, Babo."

"What's that supposed to mean? You were his mother when he abandoned you and Adelina. He is not our son."

"Don't you ever say that!" she suddenly shouted.

"And tonight of all nights," Giuseppe argued.

"Here. It's just down here. Eighty-Six Bedford Street," she said, pointing.

"There is no sign. Where is the name … Chumley's?" Giuseppe asked.

"Mr. Leland Chumley is not going to advertise his speakeasy to the authorities, Babo."

"Leland Chumley, another socialist. Another one who wants to ruin this country," Giuseppe said. "We came to this country to live their way of life—because it was a better way. We didn't come here to make a mess of it like we did in Italia."

"They will all be here on the night their heroes are executed. He will be here," she insisted. She took a deep breath and knocked on the door. There was no answer.

Giuseppe tried the handle. It was locked. Marianna knocked again.

Finally, the door slowly opened to reveal a somber young man, or as much of the young man as they could see through the narrow crack he allowed. "What do you want?" the man asked.

"We are here to see Stefano Mosca," Marianna said.

The young man opened the door wider, and his eyes, tearing from the inordinate amount of smoke emanating from the room, darted back and forth between them. "Does he know you?" the man asked.

"Tell him someone from Serra San Bruno is asking for him," Marianna said.

The man hesitated and then closed the door without a word.

"He's not going to let us in, *mi amore*," Giuseppe insisted. "Let's go back home."

Some rustling and unintelligible voices could be heard from behind the door.

Marianna's face brightened, and her lip quivered. "Stefano! Stefano Mosca!" she called out. "I know you are there. Come out please!"

Suddenly, the door sprang open, almost knocking them to the ground. In the doorway stood a tall, emaciated figure of a man in a suit that appeared two sizes too large. His eyes were sunken and red, his shirt yellow with age. And his beard and hair were obviously an afterthought.

"Stefano," Marianna squealed like a child. She threw her arms around him. "Oh, Stefano." She sobbed as she held him, but he remained unresponsive.

"Old lady, let me go. What do you want?" he asked. He looked at Giuseppe blankly. "What does she want?"

"She wants her son," Giuseppe replied.

"Well, he's not here," Stefano answered.

"What are you saying, my boy?" Marianna was confused. "Of course, it is you."

"I said, he is not here. Now the two of you need to leave. There are men here who will see to it you do so with bandages, or you can simply walk away. It is your choice."

"You don't mean that, my son," Marianna said, weeping as she reached to stroke his cheek. "You would not have sent me that note. You wanted me to find you."

Stefano grabbed her by the wrist and pushed her back. Giuseppe prevented her from falling, and then he went hard at Stefano in an attempt to wrestle him to the ground. In an instant, four men stepped through the doorway and assaulted Giuseppe. He staggered back and thought of retaliating.

"Don't do it, old man," Stefano warned. "No one here is in a very festive mood. This will not go well for you or the old woman. I suggest you go back where you came from. And I don't mean the rocks of San Bruno. You made that choice long ago. You are American now. How proud you must be. As for the note, I changed my mind. I don't want your filthy money." He spat on the ground.

Marianna approached him slowly, looking deeply into his eyes, hoping to find her son. She saw no trace. Finally, she raised her hand and slapped him hard across the face. "You are right. I was mistaken," she said. She turned to Giuseppe, took his arm, and led him away.

"Note? He sent you a note?" Giuseppe was incredulous.

◆

At 12:10 a.m., Nicolo Sacco, walking between two guards, marched the sixteen paces from his cell to the chair in the center of the small rotunda. After being strapped in, he shouted, "*Anarchia viva lunga!*" Long live anarchy. And then, in broken English, he continued, "Farewell, my wife and child and all my friends. Farewell, Mother." At 12:19 a.m., he was pronounced dead.

Shortly after, Bartolomeo Vanzetti's cell door was opened. He shook the hands of the two guards accompanying him and walked his twenty paces to the chamber in silence. Before sitting down, he turned to the warden and said, "I want to thank you for everything you have done for me." He then turned to address the witnesses in English: "I want to tell you that I am innocent and that I never committed any crime but sometimes some sin. I am innocent of all crime, not only of this, but of all. I am an innocent man. I wish to forgive some people for what they are now doing to me." He was pronounced dead at 12:26 a.m.

The case against Sacco and Vanzetti, though flawed, was ultimately too compelling to withstand worldwide protests and formal appeals. In spite of it all, Nicolo Sacco and Bartolomeo Vanzetti had become poster children. Italian immigrants were desperate for a compass, however misguided.

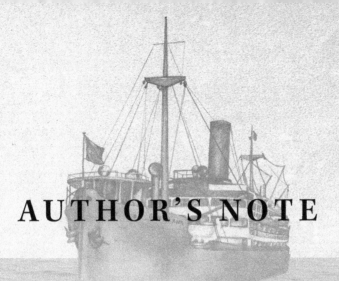

AUTHOR'S NOTE

In 1927, there were more questions than answers for those who had earlier found their way to L'America. Opportunity came at a price. And not all were willing or able to pay that price. The Italian in America stood in sharp contrast to the image being portrayed by Italy's rising star, Benito Mussolini. Ever since his march on Rome in 1922, with his chiseled face, screen-actor good looks, broad shoulders, and command of the language, he had been developing a heroic image quite different from that of the struggling, bowed figure who represented most of the transplants in the urban areas around the country.

The likes of Paolo LaChimia, Aldo Grimaldi, and Giuseppe Mosca were finally making their little marks in the new world, and then this Mussolini character came along with a virility the Italian man had not seen in quite some time. And so they were conflicted.

How each of these men and their descendants maneuvered in these waters will be the stuff of *L'America, Book Two: Adagio con Promise, 1929–1946.*

CPSIA information can be obtained
at www.ICGtesting.com
Printed in the USA
FFHW021638200719
53736172-59431FF